FAITHS IN CONVERSATION:

COMPARATIVE THEMES AND PERSPECTIVES ACROSS THE RELIGIONS

Edited by
Ruth Nicholls and Peter Riddell

Occasional Papers in the Study of Islam and Other Faiths
No. 5 (2015)

The Centre for the Study of Islam and Other Faiths
Melbourne School of Theology

mst press
Melbourne School of Theology

Occasional Papers in the Study of Islam and Other Faiths
No 5. (2015)
ISSN 1836-9782
ISBN 978-0-9924763-5-9
© 2015 Melbourne School of Theology. All rights reserved.

Editors
Ruth Nicholls and Peter Riddell

Series Editor
Peter Riddell

Production and Cover Design
Ho-yuin Chan

Publishing Services
Published by Melbourne School of Theology Press

Centre for the Study of Islam and Other Faiths
Melbourne School of Theology
5 Burwood Highway, Wantirna, Victoria 3152, Australia.
PO Box 6257, Vermont Sth, Victoria 3133, Australia
Ph: +61 3 9881 7800, Fax: +61 3 9800 0121
csiof@mst.edu.au, www.mst.edu.au

People involved in the field of Christian relations with other faiths are welcome to submit related items to the Editor for consideration for publishing in the CSIOF Occasional Papers.

iv

INTRODUCTION[1]

The concept of a multifaith society has flooded public discourse in recent decades. Multifaith groups have been formed for the purpose of better social relationships. Governments have developed policies on multifaith issues in order to enhance social harmony. In such a context, individual faiths have recognised the need to articulate views of other faiths in ways that are fresh, creative – and, especially, open and inclusive. If one examines the rapid emergence of the multifaith narrative since the last quarter of the 20th century, one could easily get the impression that multifaith societies are a new development.

Nothing could be further from the truth. Multifaith societies have existed from time immemorial. The Bible testifies to the emerging faith of the early Hebrews rubbing shoulders – and at times clashing weapons – with neighbouring faith groups, such as Canaanites, Philistines and so forth. Ancient empires such as the Greeks and Romans endorsed their own pantheon of gods, while at the same time ruling over other communities who followed significantly different expressions of faith. So the vast Roman Empire ruled over Druids in Britain, pagan worshippers of various forms in the Germanic lands, Jews in Palestine, Christians across the Roman domains, and many others. Meanwhile, further east, the various Chinese dynasties down the millennia have included within their realms followers of faiths as diverse as Confucianism, Taoism, Buddhism and Traditional Chinese Religion. They not only rubbed shoulders but also shared significant features and mutually influenced each other in most creative and interesting ways.

So the simultaneous study of multiple faiths has not only great currency in terms of present interest and relevance but it also speaks into past history in important ways. Public policy makers today can learn important lessons from the history of interaction

---

[1] Many thanks to all the contributors for the abstracts which were originally included with their papers. These have been used extensively, at times verbatim, in compiling this introduction.

1

among the faiths. In such a context, this present volume is relevant not only to current political and social discourse but also to studies of the past.

There are various approaches that can be taken to the study of multiple faiths. Comparative Religion was popular as a methodology in the mid to late 20th century. It involved students setting aside their particular faith allegiance and comparing features of different faiths to identify similarities and differences, without any implication of true or false, right or wrong. Alternatively, a Missiological Approach involves students looking at other faiths through the lens of their own, not only identifying points of difference, but also involving clear assumptions of right and wrong. A third and more recent approach is that of Comparative Theology. This involves students being transparent about their faith position but seeking wisdom from other faiths in order to find new insights into the mind of God. A fourth approach involves the setting aside of one's own faith perspective but observing and commenting on what a particular faith (not necessarily one's own) has to say about another faith.

Each of the above approaches has merit and can provide valuable insights into the multifaith world. Students of religion should not be intimidated by the considerable extent to which trend and fashion influences this field of study. In the broader academy, Comparative Religion is somewhat old-fashioned as a methodology while Missiology is shunned in secular universities as narrow and intolerant, daring to do the unacceptable by identifying beliefs of others as true or false. Such is the straitjacket imposed by the New Age West.

Nevertheless, individual volumes such as this present study cannot do everything. In the papers which follow, we will focus especially on the first and fourth approaches outlined above; i.e. Comparative Religion, as well as comments by one faith on another. In this way, we hope that we are able to assemble a set of observations on multifaith issues that will provide fresh insights into the study of four faiths: Hinduism, Buddhism, Judaism and Islam. Although all the contributors are practising Christians, this is not a study of missiology, though from time to time Christian observations will be offered on matters under discussion.

Not surprisingly, the first article in this edition of the Occasional Papers, "Faiths - a Snapshot", is an overview of the four faiths in primary focus: Hinduism, Buddhism, Judaism and Islam. It provides a valuable foundation for the subsequent papers. The papers that follow are divided into two sections. The first, and by far the larger section is concerned with *Comparing the Faiths*. Each paper presents a unique perspective based on personally selected criteria. Several of the papers compare the same concept from the perspective of two of the religions, as for example a comparison of Hinduism and Islam as in Ian Schoonwater's paper on death and dying, or Peter Riddell's article on demonic temptation in Buddhism and Islam. However some of the articles are more singular in their focus. Elizabeth Greentree's article examines the rise and development of Buddhism from its Hindu roots while providing a comparison in the process. Bernie Power takes a different perspective. He examines what the Qur'an and the Hadith have to say about Jews, a relevant topic especially in today's Middle East.

The second section, entitled *A Christian Response,* includes articles in which the writers provide a Christian response to a specific aspect, either a belief or practice as it occurs in one of the religious groups mentioned. Obviously, the topics covered are limited but they do provide an insight into possible ministry responses when a Christian encounters such an issue.

As mentioned, the paper "Four Faiths – A Snapshot", introduces a number of significant concepts to highlight the beliefs of each of the four religions in focus. Having provided a summary of these salient distinctives Richard Bath concisely details the specific understanding of 'gods, no gods or God', followed by a brief consideration of the nature of revelation as understood by each of the Faiths. That in turn leads to an overview of the character of the sacred texts which includes a brief discussion on the issue of liberation, salvation and suffering. Bath then looks at how each of the Faiths views the other. Hinduism and Buddhism tend to be pluralistic in their attitudes, while both Jews and Muslims are negative towards each other and both are negative towards Christianity. So it is a fitting introduction to what proceeds.

The first section, *Comparing the Faiths,* is introduced in another article by Bath, this time on "Hinduism and Islam". His primary concern is to compare and contrast the two religions. This he does from a number of different perspectives: their historical development, the nature of sacred revelation, doctrine of God, humanity and salvation, ethics, worship, and inter-religious context. He mentions the similarities in terms of the context of origin, methods of revelation, and compilation of sacred text. He also notes their strict roles and mutual responsibilities for maintaining social order and many worship forms while also highlighting that both often use restrictive legislation to prevent conversion to other faiths. On the other hand he points to the glaring differences. Hinduism's evolution has been very fluid and open ended, while Islam has been constricted by the authoritative weight of the Qur'an and its Hadith-dependent commentary which constitute its prophetic canon and doctrine. Also, what could be more strikingly different than Hinduism's multiplicity of gods and variation of beliefs and Islam's generally strict transcendent monotheism! Subsequently, Islam desires to have a strong and united community in submission to Allah while pluralistic Hinduism's diverse array of devotional practices and cults desire to see one's soul achieve oneness with the Supreme Reality.

One area in which these differences in terms of revelation, practice and belief are most starkly seen is in the impact on life practices, especially those that relate to death and dying. For many even these terms are to be avoided. But, in a pluralistic society where many religious practices co-exist, differing spiritual perspectives, particularly around death and dying, pose a challenge for those individuals offering end-of-life care. In dealing with "Death and Dying in Hinduism and Islam", Ian Schoonwater examines how both the Hindu and Islamic faiths treat death, what each teaches about palliative care and euthanasia, and what they teach about what lies beyond death. The next article by Ee Ling Ting fittingly follows by comparing how Hinduism and Islam view the afterlife. Ting posits that the afterlife involves the existence of a place where the dead (or their spirits) go to. It typically incorporates the idea of a god or a divine judge who judges the person according to their actions during their temporal lifetime. She identifies a graphic contrast between the Hindu belief of 'reincarnation' with Islam's graphic portrayal of both the judgment and the torments of hell on the one hand and paradise on the other.

The next five articles are somewhat more singular in the perspective they take. Each one brings their own nuanced perspective to the differences between the Faiths. Greentree examines the rise of Buddhism from its Hindu roots; Anya Kutchen, the impact of Buddhism on religions in the Chinese context; Riddell on temptation in Buddhism and Islam. After this, Power details the Muslim attitude to Jews as portrayed in the Qur'an and the Hadith; Rich Robinson examines the varying influences on Judaism; and Paul Rawson examines the emergence of New Age religion in the West.

Greentree's article observes that while Hinduism accepts Buddhism the reverse is not true. There are several reasons for that according to Greentree, who accepts Darian's thesis that Buddhism arose in response to changes in economic, political and social needs which conflicted with the Vedic traditions, especially the particularly strong emphasis on caste and the importance of the *brahman* priestly class. Thus Greentree claims that Buddhism developed and was supported as a religious ideology which would enable or at least not conflict with the necessary political and economic changes. Another reason was a rejection of doctrinal factors that could be traced back to the beginning of Hinduism, with its personal based fire-ceremonies leading to elaborate priestly rituals supported by patrons. According to Greentree, Buddhism identifies itself as a new revelation on the impermanency of all things, as well as being in opposition to both the brahmanic traditions and the harsh measures of the ascetics.

Kutchen, in her paper "The Interconnection between Buddhism and Chinese religions", reflects on the way Buddhism has not only become integrated into Chinese religions but also how Buddhism has itself been shaped by this richly varied religious and philosophical context which includes primal beliefs, Confucianism and Taoism. Such is the integration of Buddhism into Chinese life and culture that many Chinese people find it difficult to distinguish which of their beliefs and practices come from Buddhism and which come from other Chinese religions.

Riddell's article looks at another area of belief as it impacts life. In "Moments of demonic temptation in Buddhism and Islam", Riddell first outlines how the founders of both faiths, Gautama Buddha of Buddhism and Muhammad of Islam, were tempted in various ways, based on the testimony of the respective sacred texts of the two faiths. Having set the scene by relating the theme of temptation to the supreme models of the two faiths, Riddell then considers how demonic temptation is related to the masses. In this part of the discussion the attention shifts to Southeast Asia. There, the Buddhist Borobudur temple in Central Java demonstrates how the Buddha's response to demonic temptation provides a model for pilgrims who see his story carved in the walls of the temple. Also considered is an Islamic story relating the experience of death, where believers are subjected to temptation by demons seeking to divert them from their faith.

Muslims and Jews! Power, in his article, suggests that Muslim and Jewish attitudes towards each other are key to understanding the Middle East. In a detailed analysis of first the Qur'an and then the Hadith collection by Bukhari, Power delineates Muslim attitudes towards Jews under a number of headings. In terms of the Qur'an the headings are: positive views about Jews; negative views about Jews; how to treat Jews and judgement on the Jews. The final section deals with attitudes to Jews in the Hadith. In conclusion Power notes that the Qur'an takes an ambivalent attitude towards the Jewish people with some verses presenting an affirmative picture but the majority of the verses concerning the Jews take a negative view. On the other hand, the Hadith's attitude to Jews is invariably negative. Power also points out that according to Hadith accounts, Muhammad's own views towards Jews became increasingly hostile over time, to the point that he died cursing Jews and Christians.

Rich Robinson's article focuses on Judaism and makes the claim that without being impacted in various ways by other cultures, Judaism would have died. He ably demonstrates that there is no 'pure Jewish' culture, by using Levine's thesis that outside influences impact cultures at various levels and in a multitude of ways. Robinson then goes on to briefly detail ways in which the Jewish culture in many of its dimensions has been influenced by Greco-Roman culture from the beginning of the Christian period, by

Greek philosophy in the Middle Ages, together with Islam and Christianity. His article presents a perspective on Judaism that possibly isn't widely recognised.

In the final article in the section on *Comparing the Faiths*, Rawson considers the New Age Religion that has become increasingly widespread in the West. It is included in this volume because Hinduism and Buddhism underlie its beliefs and practices. The teachings of Hinduism and Buddhism around karma, the afterlife, as well as universalism and relativism were rapidly picked up by the Western world in the late 20th century. These teachings, the author claims, challenged the beliefs and teachings of the traditional Church at a time when many were questioning their beliefs. Travelling gurus and the widespread distribution of resources on Eastern Religions both facilitated the gradual emergence of the New Age Religion and continue to have an impact.

The second section titled *Christian Responses* includes three papers. Each of the papers provides a Christian response to one specific aspect of one of the other religions. The first paper by Michelle Stevens, "Pathway to Inner Peace", outlines a Christian response to the Hindu concept of karma, which is one of Hinduism's core beliefs. Fundamental to the notion of karma is that one's own actions will affect and dictate one's future. Karma is thought to control *samsara*, or the cycle of life, and determine eventual *moksha* or liberation. The basic assumption is what you reap you sow. Stevens contrasts this with the Christian belief, which teaches that salvation is a free gift, and not based on works. As such, presenting Christianity to Hindu people can be quite complicated and require patience in teaching that it is not good karma which will result in liberation, but rather by accepting the grace offered by Christ.

The next article by Kate Lim focuses on meditation, a topic that has received widespread attention during the ascendancy of New Age religion. More specifically the paper evaluates meditation in Zen Buddhism in the light of Christian teaching. Lim writes:

> Meditation is a lost art in the Christian church today. In contrast, Zen meditation has gained worldwide appeal, in part due to its inclusive nature and offer of deep spirituality without the need

for God. Religious pluralism expressed in the idea of "double belonging" among Christians who practice Zen, presents a challenge to the modern church. The two meditative traditions are, however, radically different in purpose, principles and practice. The irreducible differences are that of the necessity of God and centrality of Christ's saving work, which are excluded and rejected in Zen teaching. The quest for inner peace through meditation for Christians is ultimately not about a state of mind or consciousness, but an encounter with the living God made possible only through the saving work of Christ on the cross.

The final article in this section, "Islam: The Cross and Christ Victorious", is profoundly challenging and deals with a subject that lies at the heart of the difference between Islam and Christianity. It is the Islamic insistence that Jesus Christ did not die on the cross but that God worked deceptively so that it 'seemed that Jesus died' but was raised to heaven from where, one day he will return to establish Islam through the earth. In this essay, Brent Neely examines some of the common Islamic theological or ideological objections to the Christian doctrine of the atonement. Muslim scholars consider that the theology of redemption by the cross is irrational and altogether unworthy of Almighty God. Neely is especially concerned with the charge that cross-theology speaks of a "weak" God. In response he advocates for a more robust presentation of the 'Christus Victor' paradigm of the atonement.

The aim of this edition of the Occasional Papers has been to assemble a set of observations on multifaith issues that will provide fresh insights into the study of four faiths in particular: Hinduism, Buddhism, Judaism and Islam. Hopefully these papers will provide a better understanding of the complexities of the faith of our neighbours, as well as enabling a response that will be more sympathetic and more compassionate, as well as enhancing one's ability to relate more meaningfully to those around us.

Ruth Nicholls
Peter Riddell
December 2015

FOUR FAITHS: A SNAPSHOT

Richard Bath[2]

Within the global village that we inhabit, more than ever before Christians are exposed to diverse religious worldviews, particularly those of Hinduism, Buddhism, Judaism, and Islam.

Overview of the Faiths

Hinduism is a dynamic and ever-evolving religion.[3] Emphasis and dogma change almost as quickly as cultural currents do.[4] This is unsurprising given the lack of a central authority and defined canon of Scripture. However, the desire for a strong national identity,[5] latent caste norms[6] and individuality maintain a powerful influence on Hindu thought and praxis.[7]

Many scholars see **Buddhism** as a reaction against the theologies and injustices prevalent in Hinduism in the mid-sixth century B.C.[8]

---

[2] Richard completed his Master of Divinity degree at MST in 2011 and currently works in the personnel team of a Christian mission agency that has people serving in Asia and the Arab World. He also has a background in Mechanical Engineering and lives in Regional Victoria with his young family.

[3] Sabapathy Kulandran, *Grace: A Comparative Study of the Doctrine in Christianity and Hinduism*, London, UK: Lutterworth Press, 1964, pp118-130. In the early Vedic texts, 33 gods "are associated with nature powers" (p119), the *Brahmanas* "set forth rules regulating worship and sacrifice"(p123), while the later *Upanishads* taught that "peace and freedom could come only through true knowledge" (p126).

[4] David Smith, *Hinduism and Modernity*, Oxford: Blackwell, 2003, pp144-145. "The gods mirror the human world" and "Indian film stars...take on the role of gods on film".

[5] David G. Burnett, *The Spirit of Hinduism: A Christian Perspective on Hindu Life & Thought*, 2nd edn., Oxford: Monarch Books, 2006, p284. The *Hindutva* movement "stresses pride in Hinduism and seeks to reclaim a dominant position for Hinduism in Indian cultural, religious, and political affairs".

[6] Burnett, p277. Even amongst the Hindu Diaspora, many "have retained the practice of caste marriage".

[7] Smith, p144. "The devotee has the freedom to choose where they place their devotion."

[8] Gunapala Dharmasiri, 'Extracts from A Buddhist Critique of the Christian Concept of God' in *Christianity Through Non-Christian Eyes*, Paul J. Griffiths (ed.), Maryknoll, NY: Orbis Books, 1991, pp153-161. Buddha was disillusioned with "Upanishadic and other theories of soul"

Some Buddhists blame theistic revelation(s) for 'cruel practices in the name of religion'[9] and instead redirect focus onto the psychology of the individual person as the door to liberation from the physical cosmos.[10] In reflecting the experiences of its founder, Buddhism thus places great emphasis on personal morality[11] and the emptying of the mind of harmful desires to become transcendent of any existence.[12]

Like Hinduism, **Judaism** is not a static ancient religion, even though it has survived over three millennia. Political changes, particularly the destruction of the Second Temple, subsequent dispersion through foreign lands, intense persecution,[13] and adaptation to enlightenment philosophy[14] have shaped a belief system that is diverse and divergent from centuries past. Yet Judaism remains largely theocentric and ethnically united, perhaps because of ongoing affinity for participation in its ancient festivals.[15]

In many aspects, **Islam** takes strict monotheism to its logical conclusion. Its revealed word, the Qur'an, takes on divine attributes as the eternal, perfect, and unchanging manifest revelation on

---

(p154). Cf. World Council of Churches, "Buddhist Attitudes to Other Religions" in *Interreligious Dialogues* no. 49, Salzburg: WCC, 2007, p1, which notes the "anti-Vedic polemics of the early Buddhists … [and] Buddhism's virtual excommunication by Hinduism" in retaliation.

[9] K.S.D.M Thera, 'What Buddhists Believe - The God-Idea', *BuddhaSasana* http://www.zencomp.com/greatwisdom/ebud/whatbudbeliev/259.htm , cited on 16/01/2009.

[10] N. Thera, *BuddhaNet*. http://www.accesstoinsight.org/lib/authors/nyanaponika/godidea.html, cited 16/01/2009. Buddhist meditators "utilize the meditative purity and strength of consciousness for the highest purpose: liberating insight".

[11] K.S.D.M Thera. "[Man] is neither punished nor rewarded by anyone but himself according to his own good and bad action."

[12] N. Thera, *BuddhaNet*. Nibbana is "a state utterly transcending the world…, the ultimate cessation of suffering and the final eradication of greed, hatred and delusion".

[13] Stephen M. Wylen, *Settings of Silver: An Introduction to Judaism*, New York: Paulist Press, 1989, pp175-206.

[14] Wylen, pp263-269. The Pre-eminent Jewish Enlightenment scholar, Moses Mendelsohn (1729-1786), was instrumental in redefining Judaism as "a philosophy and a religion … [expressing] the liberal ideals of the modern age [and] a confession of faith in the one God." p265.

[15] Herman Wouk, *This is My God: The Jewish Way of Life*, Garden City, NY: Doubleday, 1959, p86. As a people who have survived so much disaster, Jews recognize the importance of maintaining community identity in their festivals. Wouk sees the theological link: "The Jew orders all his acts on the hypothesis that God is there, so he is a hopeful man. Acting on that hypothesis, he has lasted a very long time".

10

Earth.[16] In concert with the text, Islam perceives Allah as a unity who is essentially unknowable[17] yet feared as a stern judge.[18] It is subsequently militant in its condemnation of real or perceived polytheism, the religion that was dominant during Muhammad's life.[19] A strong undercurrent of fatalism is apparent, as Allah's sovereignty and omnipotence are central, while human potency and individual autonomy are necessarily repressed.[20] Yet diversity within Islamic belief and practice are readily apparent. Elements of folk religion, mysticism, theocracy, and the importance of social and ethnic cohesion all broaden its reality and appeal.

God across the Faiths

All four religions explore the topic of the Ultimate Reality. Sabapathy Kulandran examines the shifting views of God within **Hinduism** over centuries past. In the ancient Vedic texts (1500-1000BC), the conception of "God" is not defined as a unified deity, but rather a competition between gods vying for supremacy, not unlike those seen in many of the epics of the Ancient Near East.[21] This is particularly apparent since the sky god 'Varuna loses his place to Indra, the god of thunder'.[22] The question of God remained in the shadows during the time of the *Brahmana* texts (900-700BC), but the later *Upanishad* texts (800-400BC) brought a

---

[16] Ignaz Goldziher, *Introduction to Islamic Theology and Law*, trans. A. & R. Hamori, Princeton, NJ: Princeton, 1981, p97. The orthodox dogma is that "the Qur'an being the revelation that ... did not originate in time... has existed in all eternity. The Qur'an is uncreated".

[17] Daud Rahbar, *God of Justice: A study in the Ethical Doctrine in the Qur'an*, Leiden, UK: E.J.Brill, 1960, p8. "What is the Qur'an's conception of God? To this no scientific answer has been given so far."

[18] Rahbar, p5. "Fear of God is the dominant sentiment in Qur'anic morality. The roots of this sentiment are in God's stern justice".

[19] Andrew Rippin & Jan Knappert, 'A Popular Theological Statement', in *Textual Sources for the Study of Islam*, Chicago, Il: Chicago University, 1986, p128. "God's sixth necessary quality is His unity or uniqueness in essence, in substance, and in activities, i.e. the absence of plurality." Note also Q2:165, Q3:151, Q5:72-73, Q9:5.

[20] W. Montgomery Watt, *Free Will and Predestination in Early Islam*, London, Luzac & Co, 1948, p169. Watt sees the root of this fatalism in the Qur'an's restoration of the idea that "It is not by impersonal, unfeeling Time that man's life is determined, but by God".

[21] Alberto Green, *The Storm-god in the Ancient Near East*, Winona Lake, IN: Eisenbrauns, 2003, pp188-189. The Hittite storm-god Teshub ascends the throne as King of the Cosmos after a struggle with Kumarbi. Similar battles are apparent in the Canaanite El/Yam/Baal myths.

[22] Kulandran, p121.

theistic understanding of Brahman back into focus yet identified both God and the soul (*atman*) as One.[23] This is a more monistic (rather than theistic) concept of God. Consequently 'the Absolute could not be an object of worship',[24] thus ushering in a plethora of personal and incarnated gods such as Vishnu, Siva, Brahma, and their many offspring and cohorts as deities to be worshipped; this situation remains prevalent today.

Buddhism's rejection of theism originates as a consequence of its insistence on eliminating any desire or 'craving for existence'[25] who is 'represented ... by an eternal, omnipotent God or godhead'.[26] N. Thera accuses theism of having 'stood against science and the advancement of knowledge, leading to ill-feelings, murders and wars... [and] failed in their attempt to enlighten mankind.'[27] This view is not dissimilar to the conclusions of Richard Dawkins and other so-called *New Atheists* who fervently espouse an anti-religious polemic at the popular level. Ironically, Buddhism's rejection of the idea of the eternal soul and embrace of the power of consciousness is adopted by modern *Meme Theory*, an attempt by scientific naturalists like Dawkins to explain religious thoughts and delusions of God as 'mental viruses'.[28]

Judaism, the oldest of the Abrahamic faiths, relies on the revelation of 'the hidden unknown God ... [showing] Himself to man'[29] to deny polytheism, pantheism, syncretism, dualism, and pagan conceptions of God.[30] The common revelation of God in Judaism and Christianity via the Old Testament gives a remarkably similar narrative interpretation of God in history; the living God who created the earth, will judge and save the world in righteousness, and fulfil His purposes in the new heavens and new earth.[31] Yet

---

[23] Kulandran, p127.

[24] Kulandran, p137.

[25] N. Thera, *BuddhaNet.*

[26] N. Thera, *BuddhaNet.*

[27] N. Thera, *BuddhaNet.*

[28] Richard Dawkins, *The God Delusion,* London, UK: Bantam Press, 2006, p218.

[29] Jacob J. Ross, 'Revelation', in *Encyclopaedia Judaica*, (22 vols), 2nd edn.; F. Scolnik & M. Berenbaum; (ed.), Macmillan, 2007, vol 17, p253.

[30] Lou H. Silberman, 'God', in *Encyclopaedia Judaica* (22 vols), 2nd edn., vol 7. p653.

[31] Silberman, pp654-655.

Judaism rejects the Christian doctrine of the Trinity based upon their view that it is 'a denial of the divine unity'.[32]

Islam rejects the accuracy and veracity of the Jewish and Christian scriptures largely because the Qur'an is considered as the final, eternal, and authoritative revelation,[33] and 'God has not left another proof after His book'.[34] Francis Peters posits the throne verse (Q2:255) as expressing Allah's eternal sovereignty and omniscience, which motivates earthly kings and rulers into submission.[35] Therefore, many Muslims feel that their faith is vindicated as true and right when Islamic rule is established.

However, inconsistencies persist. Prominent evangelical apologist Norman Geisler is deeply critical of the Islamic tendency towards agnosticism because Muslims worship 'a God who is basically unknowable'[36], since only his will is revealed, not his essence. The problem of evil also haunts Islamic theology, since both good and evil originate from Allah.[37]

Views of other Faiths

Pluralism, defined by Jay Lakhani as 'an acceptance that there can be many pathways for making spiritual progress',[38] is the core value espoused by many who speak for modern **Hinduism**. Sue Menon remarks that 'diverse religious practices within Hinduism'[39]

---

[32] Silberman, p670.

[33] Goldziher, p97.

[34] A. Rippin & J. Knappert, 'The Letter of Al-Hasan Al-Basri' *in Textual Sources for the Study of Islam*, p117.

[35] Francis E. Peters, *Judaism, Christianity and Islam: The Classical Texts and Their Interpretation* (3 vols); Princeton, NJ: Princeton University Press, 1990, vol. 2, pp50-51.

[36] Norman Geisler, *Answering Islam: The Crescent and the Cross. Problems of Islamic Monotheism*, (2nd edn.,) Grand Rapids, MI: Baker Books, 2002, p141. Geisler blames this agnosticism for the near deification of Muhammad within some sects of Islam, even though such assessment is rejected by orthodox Muslims.

[37] Q4:78 "...If some good befalls them, they say, "This is from Allah"; but if evil, they say, "This is from thee" (O Prophet). Say: "All things are from Allah."..."

[38] J. Lakhani, 'True Pluralism for a Truly Pluralistic Society', *Hinduism Today* April/May/June 2008, http://www.hinduismtoday.com/archives/2008/4-6/63_pluralism.shtml, cited 16/03/2009.

[39] S. Menon, 'Multiculturalism from a Hindu Perspective', *Sulekha*, http://suesinbox.sulekha.com/blog/post/2008/06/multiculturalism-from-a-hindu-perspective.htm, cited on 17/02/2009.

permit this pluralistic outlook. From a practical angle, Swami Nikhilananda promotes the goal of finding 'a universal philosophy, a universal mythology, or a universal ritual'[40] as the means to 'eliminate religious friction',[41] and sees dogmatic theologies which compete polemically against others as the barrier. Instead, he argues, the experience of 'God consciousness'[42] within each religion should become the overriding concern in each of them. However, efforts to promote such tolerance for the "other" have been enshrined in Indian anti-conversion laws which are used as a vehicle to oppress missionary religions.[43] It's a somewhat tragic outcome since Mahatma Gandhi himself was said to be 'incapable of discriminating against anyone on account of religion, race, caste, colour or anything'.[44] With subsequent partition and deep mistrust between India and its neighbours, maintaining Hindu identity thus remains an important bulwark.

Many **Buddhist** commentators take a similar view to pluralistic Hindus by trying to focus on similarities rather than differences and even adopting some of their practices.[45] Yet they admit theological differences. The relationship between Buddhism and Islam is perhaps the most antagonistic. Alexander Berzin surveys this history, from the subjugation of Buddhists to '*dhimmi* status'[46] during the Umayyad and Abbasid Caliphates, to Muslims and

---

[40] S. Nikhilanandra, 'Inter-religious Attitude' in 'Understanding Hinduism'. http://www.hinduism.co.za/inter-re.htm#interreligious, cited 10/09/2007.

[41] S. Nikhilanandra.

[42] S. Nikhilanandra.

[43] US Department of State: Bureau of Democracy, 'Human Rights, and Labor', in *International Religious Freedom Report 2010: India* http://www.state.gov/g/drl/rls/irf/2010/148792.htm, cited 10/11/2010. "There were reports from some faith-based media of approximately 18 arrests under state level "anticonversion" laws and other restrictive laws in Chhattisgarh and Madhya Pradesh during the reporting period. Christian Solidarity Worldwide (CSW) reported over 50 incidents during the reporting period in which Christians were falsely accused of forcible conversions, often beaten, and arrested by police."

[44] Pascal Nazereth, *Gandhi and Islam,* Faith Conversations Chat Group email, 6 June 2007.

[45] A. Berzin, 'The Buddhist View toward Other Religions' *in The Berzin Archives* http://www.berzinarchives.com/web/en/archives/approaching_buddhism/world_today/b uddhist_view_other_religions.html, August 10, 1988, revised 1999. Some Buddhists learn social service ideas from Christians, while some Christians learn meditation and contemplative techniques from Buddhists.

[46] A. Berzin, 'A Buddhist View of Islam' in *Islam and Inter-faith Relations: The Gerald Weisfeld Lectures 2006*, Lloyd Ridgeon and Perry Schmidt Leukel -(eds), London: SCM Press, 2007, pp225-51.

Tibetans coexisting in separate communities during the 17th century.[47] A perceived Buddhist *live-and-let-live* approach has its limits: when Buddhists perceive religious fervour and/or political independence amongst people of other faiths there can be brutal suppression as seen with the Muslims in Southern Thailand[48] and Burma, and Christians in Burma and Laos.[49]

Jews have lived besides both Christians and Muslims since those two faiths began, but the relationship has rarely been a peaceful one. Jewish experience of Christendom, particularly when it was militarily and politically dominant, has led them to regard Christian beliefs as heretical, false, and idolatrous.[50] Efforts in recent decades to improve relations between Christians and Jews, with statements such as *Nostra Aetate* and *Dabru Emet*, have had a tangibly positive impact, yet there has equally been capitulation from many in both faith communities to promote pluralism[51] and abandon evangelism.[52]

The vicious anti-Semitic tirades of the notorious Islamist Sayyid Qutb[53] repeatedly draw upon the 1905 Russian forgery *The*

---

[47] Berzin: The Muslims had fled from famine into Tibet and the 5th Dalai Lama tolerated their presence in the land. However, the Muslims lived separately under their own Shari'a laws.

[48] US Department of State: Bureau of Democracy, 'Human Rights, and Labor', in *International Religious Freedom Report 2010: Thailand.*
http://www.state.gov/g/drl/rls/irf/2010/148897.htm, cited 10/11/2010. Much of the violence has occurred between various Muslim factions; however violent attacks between ethnic Malay Muslims and Thai Buddhists have been common and show no sign of abating.

[49] US Department of State: Bureau of Democracy, 'Human Rights, and Labor', in *International Religious Freedom Report 2010: Laos.*
http://www.state.gov/g/drl/rls/irf/2010/148878.htm, cited 10/11/2010. In Laos, Christians have been regularly imprisoned for refusing to recant their faith, and proselytism is outlawed.

[50] R.J. Zwi Werblowsky, 'Christianity' in *Encyclopaedia Judaica*, (22 vols), vol. 4, pp670-679. It was considered a heretical sect from the beginning, but idolatrous when it adapted the cultic iconography it used during the middle ages; p678.

[51] T. Frymer-Kensky, D. Novak, P. Ochs, & M. Signer, 'Dabru Emet', in *Jews and Christians: People of God*, C.E. Braaten & R.W. Jenson (ed.) Grand Rapids, MI: Eerdmans, 2003, p181. "Neither Jew nor Christian should be pressed into affirming the teaching of the other community".

[52] Dan Cohn-Sherbok, *The Crucified Jew: Twenty Centuries of Christian Anti-Semitism,* Grand Rapids, MI: Eerdmans, 1992, p228. 'Lord Coggan, formerly archbishop of Canterbury [said] ...'The tragedy takes place when mission or evangelism is interpreted in terms of proselyzation."

[53] Sayyid Qutb, 'Our Struggle with the Jews', *in Past Trials and Present Tribulations: A Muslim Fundamentalist's View of the Jews,* trans. R. Nettler; Oxford: Pergamon Press, 1987, pp76-80. Qutb sees Jews in a worldwide conspiracy to undermine Islam.

Protocols of the Elders of Zion and could easily be dismissed as a reaction against the creation of the modern state of Israel at the expense of Arab rule in Palestine. But given the depth of anti-Jewish sentiment in the Qur'an[54] and the enmity between Jews and **Muslims** during Muhammad's lifetime,[55] Qutb's perspective isn't unique, innovative, or heretical.

The moderate voices of Muhammad Talbi and Fazlur Rahman are diplomatic in their views of Christians and Jews and implicitly admit the failure of Muslims to create 'the best community'[56] in the modern world. Talbi sees the common challenge of secularism as the problem, and urges modern Muslims to take a more dynamic approach in exegeting the Qur'an similar to how Christians confront secularism.[57]

Rahman recognizes the irreconcilable differences between Christian and Islamic theology,[58] as do others involved in interfaith dialogue, and demands a rejection of claims of exclusivity if dialogue is to proceed and be fruitful.[59]

However, at the popular level, voices for moderation within Islam appear to be rather silent. Instead, polemical tracts such as an anti-Buddhist tract by Harun Yahya[60] are widely distributed, with Qur'anic suras denouncing pagan religion and expressing strict

---

[54] Examples are Q5:82 "You will surely find the most intense of the people in animosity towards the believers [to be] the Jews...". , Q5:64 referring to the Jews: "Chained are their hands, and cursed are they...", and Q2:96 "And you will surely find them the most greedy of people for life..."

[55] Sayyid Abul A'la Mawdudi, *Towards Understanding the Qur'an*, vol. 1, Leicester: The Islamic Foundation, 1988, p280. Mawdudi in his commentary on Q3:118 claims that in Medina the newly-converted Muslims maintained good relations with the Jews but blames "the hostility of the Jews towards the Arabian Prophet" for destroying and ending the friendship.

[56] Fazlur Rahman, 'The People of the Book and the Diversity of Religions', in *Major Themes in the Qur'an*, Minneapolis, MN: Bibliotheca Islamica, 1980, p107. Rahman quotes Q3:110 here but argues this verse is not an assurance.

[57] Muhammad Talbi, 'Islam and Dialogue: Some Reflections on the Current Topic', in *Christianity Through Non-Christian Eyes*, Paul J. Griffiths (ed.), Maryknoll, NY: Orbis Books, 1991, pp82-101.

[58] Rahman, "The unacceptablity of Jesus' divinity and the Trinity to the Quran is incontrovertible", p109.

[59] Rahman, p106.

[60] Harun Yahya, *Islam and Buddhism*, trans. R. Evans, New Delhi: Islamic Book Service, 2003.

monotheism superimposed over images of Buddhist idolatry and nature.

Conclusion

All of the four non-Christian faiths reflected upon in this paper have been significantly shaped by the everyday experiences of humanity, real or perceived Revelations of God, and the desire for liberation and salvation from suffering and oppression. Essential differences between each religion are largely irreconcilable and should be recognized as such.

PART ONE

COMPARING THE FAITHS

HINDUISM AND ISLAM

Richard Bath

Introduction

Hinduism and Islam are the two faiths that dominate the religious landscape of South Asia. From a Western perspective, these religions have much in and yet also much in stark contrast. This paper compares and contrasts these religions in the fields of historical development, sacred revelation, doctrine of God, humanity and salvation, ethics, worship and finally inter-religious context.

Origins and Development

Unlike Qur'anic Islam which entered the world in the 7th Century A.D., Hinduism is a religious tradition which 'is the product of 5000 years of development'.[1] Archaeological excavations in the Indus Valley river complex in both India and Pakistan have given substantial insight into its origins. Religious rituals involving 'ceremonial ablutions',[2] alongside sacred 'rivers of life',[3] characterized an essential link with the local geography. In contrast, Islam's origins in the arid regions of western Arabia place it in a different geographic context, although water located in various oases were essential for the survival of its inhabitants.[4]

The history of the Indus Valley is subject to considerable speculation. Some have argued that the early 'Semito-Negroid civilization of the Indus Valley was destroyed by barbaric Vedic

---

[1] Raymond Hammer, 'The Eternal Teaching: Hinduism' in *The World's Religions* (rev. edn.), Pat Alexander (ed.), Oxford: Lion Books, 1994, p170.

[2] Raymond Hammer, 'Roots: The Development of Hindu Religion' in *The World's Religions* (rev. edn.), p173.

[3] Hammer, 'Roots' p173.

[4] Hans Küng, *Islam: Past, Present & Future*, trans. J. Bowden, Oxford: Oneworld, 2007, p27.

Aryan nomadic hordes'[5] from the North-East. Those more sympathetic to traditional Hinduism contend that there was no Aryan invasion and that such people 'have been in the region ... much earlier than proposed'.[6] What is clear, is that the Indus Valley region (where Hinduism began) existed at the intersection of religious influences from various quarters of Asia.

The Arabian Peninsula has always been sparsely populated given its arid landscape, and various ethnic groups have occupied it in ancient times; influencing the outlook of the earliest Muslims.[7] The pre-Islamic Ka'bah in Mecca contained 360 idols, and there is some debate whether *Hubal*, the moon god,[8] or *Allah* was considered the chief henotheistic deity.[9] It is understood that some of the deities were female goddesses, some of whom the Qur'an identifies:

> *So have you considered al-Lat and al-Uzza?*
> *And Manat, the third – the other one? (Q53:19-20)*

The earliest Hindu scriptures, the *Rig Veda* (middle of second millennium BC) 'praise a pantheon of deities, of whom the most important is undoubtedly Indra, ... an active, powerful, unpredictable, combative god'.[10] What can be construed as theistic aspects of Indra's deity are obvious,[11] yet Varuna, the sky god, probably best equates to *Lord of the Heavens*, 'the keeper of the cosmic order'.[12] Therefore, early Hindu henotheism was not far removed in many respects from the pantheon of gods worshipped in Arabia before the emergence of Islam.

---

[5] David Burnett, *The Spirit of Hinduism: A Christian Perspective on Hindu Life and Thought,* 2nd edn.; Oxford: Monarch Books, 2006, p24. Dalit Indians generally support this theory as it sees them as victims of Aryan invaders who were the ancestors of today's higher caste Indians.

[6] Burnett, p23.

[7] Küng, p32. Byzantine Christians, Jews, Ethiopians, Sabeans, Persians, and others had a considerable presence in pre-Islamic Arabia.

[8] Karen Armstrong, *Islam: A Short History,* New York: Random House, 2000, p11.

[9] Küng, p80.

[10] Richard H. Davis, 'A Brief History of Religions in India' in *Religions of India in Practice,* Donald .S. Lopez; (ed.), Princeton, NJ: Princeton University Press, 1995, p8.

[11] *Rig Veda* 2.12.7.
"He under whose supreme control are horses, all chariots, the villages, and cattle;
He who gave being to the Sun and Morning,
who leads the waters, He, O men, is Indra."

[12] Rajendra P. Pandeya, 'The Vision of the Vedic Seer' in *Hindu Spirituality: Vedas through Vedanta,* Krishna Sivaraman (ed.), New York: Crossroad Publishing, 1989, p22.

Even after the Vedas were written in Sanskrit, Hinduism evolved continuously (and continues to), as a core presumption of Hinduism is that spiritual insight is ongoing. The first millennium B.C saw the sacrificial system elaborated upon by the *Brahmanas*, and philosophical and moral concerns discussed in the later *Upanishads* which 'centred around the individual pursuit of liberation through austerity and knowledge'.[13] Folkloric epics of ancient battles involving the gods form theological narratives and parables so important for the devotional lives of Hindus continue to emerge.[14] Even today the Hindu religion itself continues to evolve in the fast moving currents of modernism, technology, immigration, and urbanization.[15]

Islam itself has seen a multitude of sects and divisions occur over its history, ranging from the liberal Mu'tazilites who were influenced by Greek philosophy to the extremely puritanical Kharijites and Wahhabis of earlier and later periods.[16] The religious conservatives have prevailed in many regions, particularly in Islam's heartland of Saudi Arabia.[17] Meanwhile, attempts at secularization as occurred in modern Turkey have resulted in some re-interpretation of Islamic traditions,[18] but even so awareness of Islamic identity remains strong and resists conceding significant ground to non-Muslim faiths.[19]

Revelation & Canon

---

[13] Davis, p14.

[14] Raymond Hammer, 'Concepts of Hinduism' in *The World's Religions*, (rev. edn.), p192.

[15] Davis, p51. "Though historically grounded, Indian religions remain alive to their modernity, to their new political settings, the new international audiences, and the new possibilities of technology in the modern world."

[16] Küng, p186.

[17] Küng, pp459-460. Ironically, 85% are in favour of political reform yet 59% still support the religious establishment in Saudi Arabia.

[18] D. Jones, 'Challenging Traditional Gender Roles' in *Qantara.de*. http://en.qantara.de/Challenging-Traditional-Gender-Roles/7618c7687i1p486/, cited 12 Aug, 2005. The Turkish Religious Affairs Directorate (or Diyanet) appointed 450 women as preachers in Turkish mosques.

[19] Küng, p46. "The Christian minority ... leads a miserable life and is legally insecure; officially it does not exist".

Both Islam and Hinduism have scriptures they consider as revelation from God, but are somewhat different in form and source of authority. Hinduism does not have a canon of Holy Scripture per se.[20] Rather, it includes a vast array of books of different genres including 'philosophical treatises, folk medicine, erotic poetry, and grammar tomes, as well as devotional hymns, liturgical manuals, and ethical instructions'[21] which have been compiled and collected over many centuries.

The *Rig Veda* which most scholars date to the 2nd millennium B.C, consists of over one thousand 'hymns of praise to a group of largely male deities'.[22] Their authorship is traditionally attributed to sages who had special insights and initially passed them on via recitation for many centuries.[23] Along with the *Brahmanas* and *Upanishads*, these texts are regarded as *Śruti*: heard revelations from the divine.[24] Hinduism's post-Vedic texts reflect upon and mythologize earlier history, often drawing on oral tradition. These are considered to be *smriti*, that is, memorized writings.[25]

Essential to Islamic revelation is the concept of a line of prophets from Adam to Muhammad. Many of the important figures of the Judeo-Christian narrative are referred to as *Nabi* (prophet), while Moses, David, and Jesus, with the final addition of Muhammad, are given the title *rasul* (a messenger of God) since they have 'brought his people a book'.[26] Similar to the Hindu texts, Islam's central text, the Qur'an, was also originally recited orally before manuscripts were compiled. However, human authorship is not attributed to Muhammad; rather, Muslims believe that he received direct revelations from Allah via the Angel Gabriel over a period of

---

[20] Burnett, p29.

[21] A. Bass, 'An Investigation of Hindu Scripture', in *Sakthi: An Apologetics Network in India*. http://www.sakshitimes.org/index.php?option=com_content&task=view&id=145&Itemid=42, cited 2004.

[22] Burnett, p30. Many Hindus claim pre-historic origins up to 30000 years, but there is no scholarly support of this.

[23] Burnett, p29.

[24] Warren Matthews, *World Religions* (6th edn), Belmont, CA: Wadsworth, 2010, p74.

[25] Matthews, p69. "Among the *smriti* writings are the Laws of Manu, and the Itihasa-Purana, which includes the epics of the Mahabharata and the Ramayana."

[26] Küng, p94. Moses delivered the Torah, David the Psalms, and Jesus the Gospels.

around 23 years.[27] Further, the doctrine that the Qur'an is the final revelation is contained explicitly within the text itself.[28]

Islamic tradition asserts that the definitive uncorrupted Qur'an was compiled almost twenty years after Muhammad's death by the Caliph 'Uthman in 650, who required all previous written manuscripts and copies be destroyed.[29] Yet the reliability and sources of the Qur'an have come under scrutiny in recent decades, particularly since the discovery of the San'a manuscripts in 1972. Prof. Gerd Puin who is currently examining these manuscripts asserts that 'the Koran is a kind of cocktail of texts that were not all understood even at the time of Muhammad'.[30] Nevertheless, it is difficult to dispute that the Qur'an contains 'prophetic, legislative, wisdom, narrative and hymnic'[31] types of discourse which have impacted the minds and souls of millions.

Compared to the Hindu scriptures, the Qur'an takes on a decidedly stern, legal and polemic tone. Yet both display strong emotive language, ancient wisdom, and sincere devotion to their respective deity/ies. Also, in perception the Qur'an is not dissimilar from Hinduism's *śruti* texts in being seen as sourced directly from the divine, while the Islamic *Hadith* and *Sirahs* (prophetic traditions and biographical materials) resemble the *smriti* or memorized texts in that they are later compilations of tradition.

Doctrine of God

To categorize the Hindu worldview of God as pantheistic is a matter of debate, given the variety of sects and beliefs under its broad umbrella. But the *Upanishads* do teach 'that only one God

---

[27] Küng, p530.

[28] Q5:3 "This day I have perfected for you your religion and completed favour upon you and have approved for you Islam as religion". This doesn't allow future revelations to be admitted.

[29] Al Bukhari 6:61:650 "So 'Uthman sent a message to Hafsa saying, 'Send us the manuscripts of the Qur'an so that we may compile the Qur'anic materials in perfect copies and return the manuscripts to you.'"

[30] T. Lester, 'What is the Koran' in *Atlantic Monthly* http://www.theatlantic.com/magazine/archive/1999/01/what-is-the-koran/4024/3/, cited Jan 1999).

[31] Küng, p531.

(Brahman) exists'.[32]   His impersonal and unknowable Being is taught quite explicitly:

> "There [Brahman] the eye cannot travel, nor speech nor mind. Nor do we know how to explain it to the disciples." (Kena Upanishad 1:3)

Indeed, Brahman is considered to be the one true reality:

> Meditate, and you will realize that mind, matter, and Maya (the power which unites mind and matter) are but three aspects of Brahman, the one reality." (Shvetashvatara Upanishad 1:12)

Both *Bhakti Hinduism* and the *Hare Krishna* movement reject the notion of an impersonal God,[33] and the *Bhagavad Gita* concurs when Arjuna in conversation with Krishna states:

> You are the Supreme Brahman, the ultimate, the supreme abode and purifier, the Absolute Truth and the eternal divine person (*Bhag.Gita.* 10:12).

Further, the worship of Vishnu and/or Shiva 'have a supreme personal god at their centre, to whom each asks its followers to turn'[34] and depend upon. Hinduism consists of multiple deities who are variously worshipped, with monistic undertones in the claim that 'God is all, and all is One'.[35]

Islam on the other hand has an unbending and strict monotheistic doctrine of God: "Allah — there is no deity except Him, the Ever-living, the Sustainer of [all] existence" (Q2:54). The Qur'an repetitively rails against any association or worship of other deities besides Allah[36] and condemns polytheists to eternal torment.[37] The eternally indivisible unity of God[38] and His absolute sovereign

---

[32] Norman L. Geisler, 'Hinduism, Vedanta' in *Baker Encyclopedia of Christian Apologetics*, Grand Rapids, MI: Baker, 1999, p316.

[33] Geisler, p316.

[34] Sabapathy Kulandran, *Grace: A Comparative Study of the Doctrine in Christianity and Hinduism*, London, UK: Lutterworth Press, 1964, p137.

[35] Geisler, p318.

[36] Q4:48 "He who associates others with Allah has certainly fabricated a tremendous sin."

[37] Q50:26 "Who made [as equal] with Allah another deity; then throw him into the severe punishment."

[38] Q112.

rule over creation is utterly non-negotiable and doesn't allow any exceptions.[39]

This monotheism appears to be in direct opposition to Hindu concepts of God, yet from a Christian perspective neither appreciates and understands God's essential nature. Kenneth Cragg notes that for Islam 'what God reveals is the divine will rather than the divine nature, and that the end of revelation is obedience rather than perfect knowledge'.[40] Hans Küng likewise writes that despite his revelations, Allah 'remains the inscrutable one, ... he is enigmatic'.[41] But Hinduism's pantheistic identification of "God is all, and all is God" is anathema to the Muslim view of Allah's transcendence since 'there can be no similarity between the One [God] and what flows from It [the Universe]'.[42] Because of this distance, many Muslims have resorted to Sufi mysticism to perceive experiences of God.[43] The Qur'anic phrase "We are closer to him than [his] jugular vein" (Q50:16) is often mentioned by Sufis to defend Allah's immanence, but many orthodox Muslims interpret the "We" as angels,[44] or categorize this *surah* as metaphor.[45]

Humanity & Salvation

Islamic doctrine on the origin of humanity mirrors that of the Judeo-Christian view but with several key differences. The narratives of Q2:21-39 and Q7:11-27 describe Adam as created by Allah "from clay" (Q7:12), and worshipped by all the angels except for Satan who was subsequently banished from Paradise for his

---

[39] Q59:23 "He is Allah, other than whom there is no deity, the Sovereign, the Pure, the Perfection, the Bestower of Faith, the Overseer, the Exalted in Might, the Compeller, the Superior..."

[40] Kenneth Cragg, *The Call of the Minaret,* 2nd edn.; London, UK: Collins Liturgical, 1986, pp41-42.

[41] Küng, p86.

[42] Geisler, p372.

[43] Cragg, p47. "Much mysticism has solved this problem devotionally by bringing God and the world closer together and explaining divine unity in pantheistic terms".

[44] Ibn Kathir, *Tafsir (Abridged) Q50:16* (10 vols), 2nd edn.; Trans. S.R. al-Mubarakpuri; Riyadh: Darussalam, 2003, Vol. 9, p228. "His angels are nearer to man than his jugular vein".

[45] William Chittick, *Sufism: A Short Introduction,* Oxford: Oneworld, 2000, p34. Many Sufis contend that a mysterious paradox exists and that this bewilderment and perplexity actually enables one to begin to understand God.

disobedience.[46]   Both Adam and his wife Eve lived "in Paradise" (Q7:19) but also fell from Paradise to earth because they ate from the forbidden tree.[47] Humanity's obligation, beginning with Adam, the first prophet,[48] was to seek guidance from Allah, such that whoever follows his guidance "will neither go astray [in the world] nor suffer [in the hereafter]" (Q20:124). This forms the core of Islamic understanding that submitting to Allah's guidance leads to a life of integrity and a peaceful community now, with abundant pleasures in the future afterlife.

But the Hindu Scriptures give a very different account of the origins of humanity. The *Rig Veda* states:

> *From him Virāj (the manifest world) was born; again Puruṣa (Man) from Virāj was born.*
> *As soon as he was born he spread eastward and westward o'er the earth.*
> *When Gods prepared the sacrifice with Puruṣa as their offering, Its oil was spring, the holy gift was autumn; summer was the wood.*
> *They balmed as victim on the grass Puruṣa born in earliest time. With him the Deities and all Sādhyas and Ṛṣis sacrificed.*
> (*Rig Veda* Book 10, Hymn 90, Verses 5-7)

It is generally accepted that the first human was Manu, a Noahic figure who saved humanity from a great flood. The *Mahabharata* epic says:

> *And in Manu's race have been born all human beings, who have, therefore, been called Manavas. (Sambhava Parva* Sect. LXXV, Thepur Hindu)

Further, the *Laws of Manu* discuss the origin of castes from Brahman:

> *He caused the Brahmana, the Kshatriya, the Vaisya, and the Sudra to proceed from his mouth, his arms, his thighs, and his feet* (Laws of Manu I, Vs 31)

In summary, according to Hinduism, humans came about as the result of a sacrifice by the gods and were divinely split into castes.

---

[46] Q7:11.

[47] Q2:36, 7:22-24.

[48] Q2:38-39.

The chief purpose of humanity in Hinduism is to seek fulfilment through the four *purusharthas* (meanings) which are *dharma* (righteousness), *artha* (wealth), *kama* (fulfillment of desire),[49] and *moksha* (liberation from worldly desires and bondages).[50] *Moksha* is particularly important in the light of Hindu understandings of the soul or *atman*. The *Upanishads* developed the idea that Brahman is the human inner self or *atman*, and that when knowledge of release from cyclic rebirth is realized; 'his soul becomes one with Brahman'.[51] It is also held that the mind and body constitute the *prakriti,* the physical human which is perishable.[52] Islam accepts the idea of the human soul, but it is distinct from Allah and will be physically resurrected with the body to either Paradise or Hell.[53] In contrast, Hinduism desires separation of body and soul. It seeks to see 'the release of the soul from a particular body for the purposes of rebirth until eventually the soul is freed from the necessity of rebirth'.[54] This significant divergence manifests itself in different ethical and worship philosophies, as will be discussed.

Ethics

Correct and right behaviour is of vital importance to both Hindus and Muslims. Both religions have legal codes, albeit neither universally codified,[55] to maintain community order and provide guidance for their followers. Islamic societies are traditionally guided by *shari'a* law which in secular terms 'means the road or way to a watering place, the well-trodden path which must always be followed'.[56] It doesn't just dictate personal ethics because it 'makes no distinction between religion and politics, [and is thus] ...

---

[49] Hindupedia, 'Purushartha' in *Hindupedia: the Hindu Encyclopedia.* http://www.hindupedia.com/en/Purushartha, cited Dec. 10, 2008.

[50] Hindupedia, 'Moksha' in *Hindupedia: the Hindu Encyclopedia.* http://www.hindupedia.com/en/Moksha, cited Feb. 21, 2008.

[51] Burnett, p67.

[52] V. Jayaram, 'Purusha, The Universal Cosmic Male and Prakriti, The Mother Nature' in *Hinduwebsite.* http://www.hinduwebsite.com/prakriti.asp, cited 2011.

[53] Q75, Q17:97.

[54] J. Burton-Page, 'Hindu' in *Encyclopedia of Islam* (12 vols); B. Lewis, V.L. Ménage, Ch. Pellat & J. Schacht (eds.), Leiden: E.J. Brill, 1971, vol. 3, pp458-459.

[55] Küng, p557. There is considerable variation in *fiqh* (teaching) across the main schools of Islamic jurisprudence and in different countries.

[56] Malise Ruthven, *Islam in the World* (rev. edn), London: Granta, 2006, p135.

enforced by the state'.[57]   Hinduism's guide for virtuous living is encapsulated by the concept of *dharma*. The earlier Vedic texts referred to it as 'the sacrifice ...which maintains the order of the cosmos',[58] while the *smirti dharmasastra* texts focus on duties to preserve social order 'according to sex, class, family, stage of life, and so on'.[59]

There are remarkable similarities in the scope and application of both *shari'a* and *dharma*. Both stipulate and define rules for food, ritual purity and ablutions, births, deaths and marriages, legal procedure and penalties, property, and finance.[60]   Both are patriarchal in that the male head of a family has privileges and rights that exceed that of females,[61] and prejudicial in that certain groups in society are given special punishments and denied socio-political participation either because of their caste[62] or religious beliefs.[63]   However, it should be mentioned that *Tantric Hinduism* critiques and confronts these 'Brahmanic concepts of hierarchy, purity, and sexual status'.[64]

But one key difference exists in relation to laws on social class. Islam breaks down class barriers amongst Muslims via the concept of the *Ummah* or Muslim Community. This is perhaps best demonstrated every year when both Sunni and Shi'a Muslims of

---

[57] Mark Durie, *The Third Choice: Islam, Dhimmitude and Freedom*, Melbourne: Deror Books, 2010, p50.

[58] Davis, p21.

[59] Davis, p21.

[60] Hinduwebsite, 'Subject Index Of Dharmasatras or Hindu Law Books', in *Hinduwebsite*, http://www.hinduwebsite.com/sacredscripts/hinduism/dharma/subject_index.asp, cited 2011. This source gives a large list of subjects covered by the *Dharmasatra* texts.

[61] Al Bukhari 3:48:826. The Prophet said, "Isn't the witness of a woman equal to half of that of a man?" The women said, "Yes." He said, "This is because of the deficiency of a woman's mind."

[62] *Nāradasmrti* 15.15 & 15:20. "A Kshatriya who reviles a Brahman must pay one hundred (Panas) as a fine. A Vaisya (must pay) one and a half hundred, or two hundred. A Sûdra deserves corporal punishment." And "Two persons, a Brahman and a king, are declared to be exempt from censure and corporal punishment in this world; for these two sustain the visible world."

[63] Durie, p123. "The *Dhimma* pact fixed the legal, social, and economic place of non-Muslims in the Islamic state. In return ... *dhimmis* were required to pay tribute (jizya) and other taxes..., and to adopt a position of humble and grateful servitude to it." Q9:29 is a key textual source of *Dhimmitude*.

[64] A. Hiltebeitel, 'Hinduism' in *The Encyclopedia of Religion* (16 vols.), M. Eliade (ed.), New York: Macmillan, 1987, vol. 6, p352.

different nationality, ethnicity, and financial status descend upon Mecca for the annual *Hajj* or pilgrimage.[65] While it is remarkable that Bedouin sheep herders can worship alongside multimillionaire businessmen, the reality usually falls short of the ideal; given the costs involved for pilgrims, and the *hajj* often being used as a platform for political and sectarian agitation.[66] Indeed beyond the *hajj*, there are signs Islamic society is more divided by sectarianism than ever before,[67] given the turmoil in the Middle East in the wake of the "Arab Spring".

An interesting area of overlap between Islam and Hinduism is *karma yoga*. William Chittick notes how the pathway to salvation through the observance of *shari'a* parallels the Hindu ethic of *karma yoga* 'which sets down the path of conforming to God's will through activity'.[68] However, since Hinduism sees such action as more a process of divinization[69] in contrast to Islam's eternal non-identification of human souls with the divine, such parallels are tenuous.

Worship

The devotional practices of Hindus and Muslims bear similarities in many outward forms, yet they remain vastly divergent in their focus. Islamic worship is rigidly defined by its five pillars: confession (*shahada*), prayer in community (*salat*), giving alms (*zakat*), fasting (*sawm*), and the pilgrimage to Mecca (*hajj*).[70] Given the plurality of deities and cults within Hinduism, a universally accepted and defined confession of faith doesn't exist.

---

[65] Ruthven, p7.

[66] Ruthven, pp7-10. The Saudi government controls strict quotas on the origin of pilgrims and the conditions for accommodation (from luxury hotels to a simple tent). Major disturbances by Shi'a pilgrims from Iran in 1979 and 1987 resulted in hundreds of deaths.

[67] Brian Turner, 'Baghdad after the Storm' in *National Geographic*. http://ngm.nationalgeographic.com/2011/07/baghdad/turner-text/1, cited June 2011. "Although there are still a few mixed neighbourhoods, Baghdad is no longer a model secular city of the Middle East".

[68] Chittick, *Sufism,* p61.

[69] S.S. Raghavachar 'The Spiritual Vision of Ramajuna' in *Hindu Spirituality: Vedas through Vedanta,* Krishna Sivaraman (ed.), New York: Crossroad Publishing, 1989, pp265-266. "He (the yogic) should regard action not as something belonging to himself, as part of his own life, but as forming a part of God's range of activity, as belonging to Him".

[70] David Kerr, 'The Worship of Islam, in *The World's Religions* (rev.edn.), ed. Pat Alexander, Oxford: Lion Books, 1994, pp321-324.

However prayers (usually in the form of mantras), food offerings, festivals, and pilgrimages all play a significant part of a Hindu's religious life. Yet the reason and object of worship is very different.

The Qur'an is very explicit in stating that Allah must be the object of worship[71] and that worship directed elsewhere is idolatrous and subject to Allah's wrath and judgment.[72]   But Islamic worship involves not just a vertical reverence for Allah; there are also strong incentives in the Qur'an to express acts of charity towards other Muslims, orphans, travellers, and others in need.[73]   Since each person "is an 'abd of God", a term which conveys the twin meanings of 'worshipper' and 'servant' ... the Qur'an sees body and spirit inseparably combined in the wholeness of human worship'.[74] This is consistent with Islam's view on bodily resurrection as mentioned earlier. In essence, the overriding paradigm and mindset is summed up in the meaning of Islam itself: 'submission to God'.[75]

Hindu worship has quite different goals. The early Vedic religion emphasized ritual sacrifices 'to please the gods in order to gain boons from them'.[76]   Thus personal gain in the *here and now* becomes the objective of worship. Yet returning to the widely held Hindu precept that 'the soul is the place where God and matter meet',[77] there is an objective to see the soul extricated or released 'from the body that it may dwell ... united with Siva in love'.[78]

For most Hindus, the local temple is the centre of worship, with each temple containing a chief statue which 'is the symbol of the

---

[71] Q16:36 "And We certainly sent into every nation a messenger, [saying], "Worship Allah and avoid Taghut (false objects of worship)".

[72] Q21:98 "Indeed, you [disbelievers] and what you worship other than Allah are the firewood of Hell. You will be coming to [enter] it."

[73] Q2:177 "Righteousness is in one who believes in Allah, the Last Day, the angels, the Book, and the prophets, and gives wealth ... to relatives, orphans, the needy, the traveller, those who ask, and for freeing slaves..."

[74] Kerr, p321.

[75] Kerr, p321.

[76] Burnett, p38.

[77] D. Dennis Hudson, 'Worship at Siva's Temple' in *Religions of India in Practice*, Donald S. Lopez (ed.), Princeton, NJ: Princeton University Press, 1995, p306.

[78] Hudson, p306. While not all Hindus are devotees of Siva, it is one of the two most commonly worshipped deities.

divine presence and the house in which it dwells'.[79] The mere presence of such idols is abhorrent to Islam. The primary acts of worship in Hinduism are largely individual and involve *puja* or paying respect to the god and making supplication, and *prasada* which involves offering food to the deity and then distributing it among fellow devotees.[80] Occasionally the Vedas are read by priests, which may also include the recitation of prayers and mantras. Many Hindus also conduct these activities at home shrines several times per day with 'special postures, gestures and utterances'.[81] Different Hindu cults place a wide variety of demands upon their devotees, with *bhakti yoga* practice necessarily requiring devotional worship to be absolutely obligatory, while for many others it is not.[82] Regardless, there is a general view that internalized devotion is the higher virtue in modern Hinduism.[83]

Prayer or *salat* is probably the most visible and recognizable public act of worship performed by Muslims. Highly ritualized and communal, it is orthodox practice to pray five set times per day, in a ritually clean state, facing Mecca, performing a set routine of prostrations and recitations as an act of adoration and submission to Allah, and as a commitment to the *Ummah*,[84] that is the worldwide Muslim community. Often prayers are made by individuals or small groups both at the assigned times, at other occasions and at locations other than the mosque. Remembrance of Allah through the practice of *dhikr* is also widespread, particularly within Sufism.[85]

---

[79] Raymond Hammer, 'Hindu Worship and the Festivals' in *The World's Religions* (rev. edn.), Pat Alexander (ed.), Oxford: Lion Books, 1994, p195.

[80] Hammer, p195.

[81] Hammer, p195.

[82] Jean Varenne, *Yoga and the Hindu Tradition,* trans. D. Coltman, Delhi: Motilal Banarsidass, 1989, p103. Some Hindus 'hold that Ishvara (god) remains passive once he has presided over the creation of the cosmos, so that there is no occasion to worship him in any practical sense'.

[83] 'Hindu Worship', *Hindu Online*, http://hinduonline.co/HinduReligion/AllAboutHinduism6.html, cited 2010. "Though you may perform external worship at regular intervals, let the internal worship of the Lord in your heart be constant and unbroken. Here worship attains completeness. Life is divine worship."

[84] Kerr, p322.

[85] Chittick, *Dhikr* 'involves the repetition of a name or names of God' with remembrance of God the primary objective.

Hindu prayer life centres around the recitation of mantras which have their basis in Vedic hymns and are often referred to in other sacred texts. The popular *gayatri mantra,* received at one's initiation (*diksha*) to enable the performing of 'daily obligatory (*nitya*) rituals',[86] is literally translated:

> "*May we attain that excellent glory of Savitar the God: So may he stimulate our prayers.*" (*RigVeda* 3:62:10)

Swami Vivekananda's free translation is:

> "*We meditate on the glory of that Being who has produced this universe; may He enlighten our minds.*"[87]

Further, the *Bhagavad Gita* makes clear the soteriological value of meditative prayer:

> "*I am soon the deliverer from the ocean of death and transmigration, Arjuna. Keep your mind on Me alone, your intellect on Me. Thus you shall dwell in Me hereafter.*" (B.G., 12: 7-8).

As a secondary role, mantras in yogic contexts are often used to conjure up magical supernatural powers (*siddhi*) to enable supersensitive perception and the manipulation of matter.[88] In summary, Hindu mantras exist for the purposes of gaining knowledge to assist one's release 'from the cycle of rebirth and suffering',[89] and sometimes for gaining 'power over objects and other beings'.[90]

Both Hinduism and Islam host the world's largest religious pilgrimages; the *Kumbh Mela* festival[91] and the hajj respectively.[92]

---

[86] S. Gupta, 'Mantra' in *The Encyclopedia of Religion* (16 vols.), M. Eliade (ed.), New York: Macmillan, 1987, vol. 9, p177.

[87] Swami Vivekananda, *The Complete Works of Swami Vivekanandra* (9 Vols), Advaita Ashram, 1915, vol. 1, p211.

[88] Ravi Ravindra, 'Yoga: The Royal Path to Freedom' in *Hindu Spirituality: Vedas through Vedanta,* p185. Sometimes drugs are used to induce psychic episodes and perform apparently miraculous superhuman feats. But using this power excessively is seen as potentially harmful.
[89] Gupta, p177.

[90] Gupta, p177.

[91] B. Banerjee, 'Millions of Hindus Wash Away Their Sins' in *Washington Post,* http://www.washingtonpost.com/wp-dyn/content/article/2007/01/15/AR2007011500041.html, cited Jan 15, 2007. An

They both serve the purpose of purifying souls of *karma* or sin and gaining insight from others in the community, yet the hajj places focus on the worship of Allah above all else.[93] Further, the hajj has circumambulation of the *Ka'bah* and animal sacrifice as its climax, while at the *Kumbh Mela* ritual bathing to wash away one's sins in the Ganges River is the primary activity.

Alms-giving is a feature of both religions, but it is universally obligatory and more rigidly defined in Islam. The Hindu texts don't ignore alms-giving and couch it in terms of gaining merit, often with rewards many times greater than the gift.[94] The *Purana* (c.4th century BC -1000AD) texts describe the cause and effect benefits of alms-giving and building temples.[95] However, most alms-giving has not been directed towards the poor, but paradoxically towards 'the upper class of brahman teachers and priests'.[96]

The Qur'an unambiguously commands that giving or *zakat* is obligatory.[97] Its recipients must be "the poor ... the needy and those employed for it" (Q9:60), and *zakat* funds are also to be distributed for proselytizing, releasing prisoners, paying debts, fighting jihad[98] and assisting stranded travellers. Various schools of Sunni jurisprudence also prescribe the amount which typically

---

estimated 70 million people attended the *Ardh Kumh Mela* at Allahabad in 2007, 5 million in one day.

[92] 'The Hajj by the Numbers', in *The Week*, http://theweek.com/article/index/209446/the-hajj-2010-by-the-numbers, cited Nov. 17, 2010. According to Saudi officials, 2.8 million Muslims attended the 2010 Hajj.

[93] Q2:196

[94] *The Laws of Manu* Chp. III, vs. 95: "A twice-born householder gains, by giving alms, the same reward for his meritorious act which (a student) obtains for presenting, in accordance with the rule, a cow to his teacher."

[95] *Agni Puruna* "What is the point of earning money if one does not build temples? Money is also meant to be donated as alms to brahmanas, but the punya or merit earned from building a temple is greater than the punya earned from donating alms."

[96] C.S.J. White, 'Almsgiving' in *Encyclopedia of Religion*, 16 vols, M. Eliade (ed.), New York: Macmillan, 1987, vol. 1, p214.

[97] Ed. Shi'ite understanding of *Zakat* differs in certain respects from that of Sunnis. While recognising that the Qur'an makes the payment of *Zakat* compulsory in principle, it does not specify the items on which it is compulsory, and the Shi'ite hadith collections only identify a limited number of items. (cf : S. M. Rizvi, *ZAKĀT IN SHĪ'A FIQH*, http://www.islamic-laws.com/pdf/ZAKAT_IN_SHIA_FIQH.pdf, cited 5 May, 2015.

[98] Ibn Kathir, *Tafsir (Abridged) Q9:60* (10 vols.) 2nd edn., trans. S.R. al-Mubarakpur; Riyadh: Darussalam, 2003, vol. 4, p458. The Qur'anic text contains the phrase "in the cause of Allah", which Ibn Kathir defines as "exclusively for the benefit of the fighters in Jihad, who do not receive compensation from the Muslim Treasury".

equates 'to 2.5 percent given from one's goods annually'.[99] Yet just as in Hinduism, motivation for paying *zakat* has reciprocal benefits multiplied for the giver.[100]

Similar to other modes of worship already discussed, the practice of fasting is firmly defined in Islam, but is observed in a plethora of many and varied forms within Hinduism. Examples include the dawn-to-dusk fasting every Tuesday by devotees of the *Goddess Mariamman* in Southern India,[101] the fast for the worshippers of Shiva on Mondays,[102] and the fast often performed during annual festivals such as *Krishna Janmashtami*.[103] On the other hand, the Muslim month of Ramadan 'during which all food, drink, and sexual activity are forbidden'[104] between sunrise and sunset, is a universal observance for devout Muslims with only minor variations.[105]

It is important to examine briefly the devotional aspects of Hindu and Islamic worship in the emotional sense. The widespread Hindu practice of *bhakti yoga* is intended to invoke intense emotions of love for the Supreme Reality, and yet the 'preparatory disciplines of *karma* and *jnana* [knowledge]'[106] *yoga* are necessary for achieving *bhakti* or 'the divine experience of God'[107] and his grace. For Muslims, Sufis, in particular, appeal to this Qur'anic verse: "Say: If you love God, follow me, and then God will love you" (Q3:31) to justify God's love taking them to an experience of intoxication and

---

[99] White, 'Almsgiving' in *Encyc of Religion*, p215. The *Mishkat Al-Masabih* hadith devotes 10 chapters to this topic, but the different schools of law have many and varied prescriptions as to the percentage amounts that are distributed to the causes listed in Q9:60.

[100] Q64:17. *"If you lend to Allah a goodly loan, He will multiply it for you and forgive you."* See also *Q57:11 & Q57:18.*

[101] Stephen P. Huyler, 'The Experience: Approaching God' in *The Life of Hinduism*, J.S.Hawley & V. Narayanan (ed.), Los Angeles: University of California Press, 2006, p33.

[102] Robin Reinhart, *Contemporary Hinduism: Ritual, Culture, and Practice*, Santa Barbara: ABC-CLIO, 2004, p131.

[103] Geoff Teece, *Religion in Focus: Hinduism*, London, UK: Franklin Watts, 2003, p27. Some people often only partially fast during this festival.

[104] Ruthven, p61.

[105] Michelle Boorstein, 'For many Muslims, start of Ramadan stirs up centuries-old debate between science and doctrine', *The Washington Post,* http://www.washingtonpost.com/wp-dyn/content/article/2010/08/10/AR2010081005777.html, cited Aug 11, 2010. The sighting of the crescent moon begins Ramadan, but timing can depend on astronomical calculations or when it is sighted in Mecca.

[106] Ravindra, p267.

[107] Ravindra, p268.

annihilation of 'all their human failings and limitations'.[108] However, this intensely mystical approach to worship is often opposed by Muslims of legalistic persuasion.[109]

Context and Inter-religious Relationships

Hinduism has a long tradition of pluralism and an ability to live alongside followers of other religions since Hinduism itself is anything but monolithic in the beliefs and devotional practices of those who identify with it. Even Hindus of more monotheistic persuasion, such as Swami Nikhilananda, assert that 'Hinduism has never developed the theory of a jealous God or exclusive salvation; the idea of a chosen people is alien to it'.[110] A major challenge to this pluralism came from the invasion of Islamic armies into Northern India in mediaeval times. Initial raids by Mahmud of Ghazni didn't achieve political success, but after the establishment of the Delhi Sultanate in 1193, 'many of the Hindu temples and idols were destroyed'[111] and mosques established in their place. Even today in places far from India, antagonism between both communities often manifests itself in violence.[112]

The motivation for this Islamic intolerance of other religions comes primarily from the command to: "Fight those who do not believe in Allah ... and who don't accept the religion of truth [Islam]" (Q9:29). Whether Hindus who resisted conversion should be killed or subjugated via the *jizya* tax differs amongst the various schools of Islamic jurisprudence,[113] and during the Mughal rule of Akbar (r. 1556-1605) such taxes against non-Muslims were revoked in order to lessen their antagonism.[114] Akbar also distanced himself from orthodox Islam and pursued the development of a new religion to

---

[108] Chittick, p38.

[109] Chittick, p29.

[110] S. Nikhilanandra, 'Inter-religious Attitude' in *Understanding Hinduism'*, http://www.hinduism.co.za/inter-re.htm#interreligious, cited Sept 2007.

[111] Burnett, p190.

[112] Leesha McKenny, 'Fear strikes as temple showered in bullets' in *Sydney Morning Herald*, March 30, 2011. The Sri Mandir Hindu temple in Auburn (Sydney) was peppered with eight rounds of bullets on March 19, 2011.

[113] Durie, p124. The Hanafi school which is dominant in India takes a less hardline approach. The Qur'an states that only people of the book (Christians and Jews) have the option of dhimmi status, yet Muhammad accepted *jizya* from the Zoroastrians.

[114] Burnett, p193.

'synthesize the world's faiths into a single religion'.[115]   Yet this attempt at pluralism failed to gain much traction and later, rulers reinstituted a more traditional application of Shari'a law. This institution remained until 1857 and was abolished in India with the imposition of British colonial rule.[116]

Since independence in 1947, the relationship between Muslims and Hindus in Pakistan and India remains deeply fractured. Partition and ongoing violence over disputed regions (i.e. Kashmir) has fermented fundamentalism on both sides.[117] The response by the more moderate is to appeal to the pluralistic realities of a diverse Hinduism,[118] and allow separate legal codes for family law.[119] However, some provincial governments in India see non-Hindu religions as a threat to Hindu identity and have introduced anti-conversion laws[120] which undermine religious freedom; an approach not dissimilar in intention to Islam's harsh penalty[121] for apostasy.[122]

Conclusion

Western mindsets often struggle to come to terms with understanding differences and similarities between Hinduism and Islam, and this paper is far from comprehensive regarding this

---

[115] Burnett, pp193-194. Akbar himself was considered a heretic by most Muslims.

[116] Küng, pp400-401.

[117] Three of the most well-known examples include the demolition of the Babri Mosque in 1992 by Hindu Nationalists, the targeted burning of a train at Godhra carrying Hindu pilgrims, and the Mumbai terror attacks of 2008.

[118] S. Menon, 'Multiculturalism from a Hindu Perspective' in Sulekha, http://suesinbox.sulekha.com/blog/post/2008/06/multiculturalism-from-a-hindu-perspective.htm, cited 2008.

[119] Werner Menski, *Modern Indian Family Law,* Richmond, UK: Curzon Books, 2001, p5.

[120] United States Commission on International Religious Freedom, 'Annual Report 2011', http://www.uscirf.gov/images/book%20with%20cover%20for%20web.pdf (2011), pp250-252.

[121] Al-Bukhari 9:83:17. Narrated 'Abdullah: Allah's Apostle said, "The blood of a Muslim who confesses that none has the right to be worshipped but Allah and that I am His Apostle, cannot be shed except in three cases: In *Qisas* for murder, a married person who commits illegal sexual intercourse and the one who reverts from Islam (apostate) and leaves the Muslims."

[122] Sayyid Mawdudi, *Towards Understanding the Qur'an (Abridged)* (6 vols), trans. Z.I. Ansari, Leicester, UK: The Islamic Foundation, 1988, vol. 1, p199. In his commentary on Q2:256 "There is no compulsion in religion" he states that this lack of compulsion is relevant for "embracing [Islamic] belief", and does not make reference to leaving it.

important topic and its impact on geo-politics today. There are significant similarities in that both faiths originated within multicultural henotheistic environments. Methods of revelation and compilation of their scriptures have certain parallels. Their societies define strict roles and mutual responsibilities to maintain social order, and many of their worship forms bear striking resemblances to one another. Both also often employ restrictive legislation to prevent conversion to faiths other than their own.

Yet their differences remain acute. Hinduism's evolution has been far more fluid and open-ended, while Islam is highly constricted by the authoritative weight of its scriptural canon and dogma. Islam places paramount importance upon its prophets and their example and the message they received, something absent from Hinduism. While Hinduism has a multiplicity of gods and variation of beliefs within a pantheist/monist paradigm, Islam's strict monotheism perceives Allah as transcendent and unable to be symbolized by any idol or image. This pantheistic/transcendent monotheistic divide produces highly divergent understandings of the human soul and body, and its destiny. Thus the desire to have a strong and united Islamic community in submission to Allah contrasts vividly with Hinduism's diverse array of devotional practices and cults to see one's soul achieve oneness with the Supreme Reality. This tends to create religious cultures that instil monolithic and pluralistic worldviews and attitudes respectively, notwithstanding the deep sectarian divisions which remain in Islam.

Whether Islam and Hinduism can peacefully coexist in the global village remains uncertain. This raises important questions for Christian engagement with both faiths.

DEATH AND DYING IN HINDUISM AND ISLAM[1]

Ian Schoonwater[2]

The Sanctity of Life

Hindu and Muslim views on death have many similarities and yet in other aspects they are poles apart. Both faiths have a strong view on the sanctity of life, and believe that life is precious and needs to be protected and preserved, but when it comes to preserving the life of one with a terminal condition, there is a conundrum.

To the Hindu the central belief of *sanatana dharma* guides the good life. This is tied to k*arma*. To honour these laws, life must be preserved,[3] but this is held in tension with the teaching that eventually a person's body has served its purpose. The body is like a set of clothes that the soul removes before putting on a new set.[4] The real self is the soul and its existence is eternal. The *Bhagavad Gita* (2.27) explains it: *"One who has taken birth is sure to die, and after death, one is sure to take birth again."*

Similarly, the Qur'an teaches that this life is temporary, and death is the transition to the next life. The Qur'an sees this life as being a test in preparation for the life to come. Allah is the one who gives life and takes it away: "He created death and life that he might put you to the proof and find which of you acquitted himself best. He is the mighty, the forgiving One." (Q67:2)[5]

---

[1] This article was first published in the *CSIOF Bulletin*, issue 4, 2011, pp82-90.

[2] Ian Schoonwater is the Senior Chaplain of Jericho Road (Presbyterian Church) and also a chaplain at the Children's Hospital at Westmead. He is currently completing his M.A. at MST and is researching the topic "Christian and Islamic voices of hope in Paediatric Palliative Care."

[3] N. Nimbalkar, 'Euthanasia: The Hindu Perspective', *National Seminar on Bio Ethics*, 24th and 25th January 2007, www.vpmthane.org, cited 25th May 2011.

[4] S. Thrane, "Hindu End of Life", *Journal of Hospice and Palliative Nursing*, vol 12, no. 6 November/December 2010, p338.

[5] All quotations from the Qur'an in this paper are taken from N.J. Dawood (trans.), *The Koran*, London: Penguin, 1990.

Beliefs on palliative care

In both faiths death is not regarded as something to be feared. For the Hindu it is just another process; for the Muslim it is the will of Allah.

The Hindu belief is that the soul goes on beyond death. The *Bhagavad Gita* (2:20) explains: "You were never born; you will never die. You have never changed; you can never change. Unborn, eternal, immutable, immemorial, you do not die when the body dies." This gives the Hindu comfort.

For the Muslim, because of the promise of paradise, death should be prepared for, but not feared:

> *As for those who say, "Our Lord is God," and take the Straight Path to him, the angels will descend to them saying "Have no fear and do not grieve; but rejoice in the   Paradise you have been promised." (Q 41.30)*

In Hinduism, the ultimate goal is to achieve *moksha*. The Hindu longs for liberation from the cycles of incarnations. To the Hindu the most important event in their life is their death.[6] The state one dies in will impact the destination of their soul; hence there is a strong focus on the state of mind as death approaches. The *Bhagavad Gita* (8.6) refers to it in this way:

> *"Whatever state of being one remembers when he quits his body ... that state he will attain without fail."*

In providing spiritual care to a terminal Hindu patient, the focus needs to be upon ensuring their mind is filled with thoughts of God. If they can't do this, then others can chant and read aloud from Hindu scriptures engaging the sense of hearing.[7] Most hospital units can usually make provision for these needs.

---

[6] For the Hindu, their death is an even more important event than their birth. It is because their death will determine where their future lies. In a pastoral care context caring for a dying patient has more significance than the care of a new mother and her baby.

[7] An interview with Henry Dom, 'Vaisnava Hindu and Ayurvedic Approaches to the care of the Dying', in *Innovations in End of Life Care* http://www2.edc.org/lastacts/archives/archivesNov99/intlpersp.asp, cited 25th April, 2011.

There are mixed views within Hinduism about palliative care. To most Hindus being kept alive on a machine or by other aggressive medical intervention will be viewed as interfering with *karma* and inhibiting the natural course of death, thus leading to a bad death.[8.] The desire to be alert until death is important to the Hindu, and there is often reluctance to receive large doses of pain relief. To some Hindus the endurance of pain is seen as having *karmic* benefits.

In Islam there is a strongly held belief that only Allah decides when someone is to die:

> "*God alone has knowledge of the Hour of Doom. He sends down the abundant rain and knows what every womb contains. No mortal knows what he will earn tomorrow; no mortal knows where he will breathe his last.*" Q 31:34

As part of submission to the will of Allah, death ought not be fought, but rather accepted as the overall divine plan.[9] When a Muslim is near death, friends and family ought to gather and give comfort, and remind them of Allah's mercy and forgiveness. They may recite verses from the Qur'an, give physical comfort, and encourage the dying one to recite words of remembrance and prayer. An important hope for a Muslim is that their last words be the *Shahadah* (the creed). The Prophet taught that sick people are very close to God and their prayers are answered.[10] The dying person should also seek forgiveness and offer it.

The approach to caring for the terminally ill and the decisions about continuing or withdrawing treatment will be influenced by patients' worldviews. In both faiths decisions regarding ongoing healthcare are seen as family decisions. For many Muslims, especially in Arabic countries, there is a preference for medical practitioners to communicate with the family before the patient, especially when communicating bad news.[11] In Hinduism, the

---

[8] Thrane, p338.

[9] Aziz Sheikh, 'Death and Dying - a Muslim perspective', *Journal of the Royal Society of Medicine*, vol. 91, March 1998, p138.

[10] K. Salman and R. Zoucha, 'Considering Faith within Culture when caring for the terminally ill Muslim patient and family', *Journal of Hospice and Palliative Care Nursing*, vol. 12, no.3 May/June 2010, p160.

[11] Salman, p161.

person is viewed as comprised of mind, body, soul, in the context of family, culture and environment. Thus the family has an important role in decisions regarding health care.

Both religions value the family gathering around and remaining with the dying person. It is not uncommon to have a continual flow of visitors or large groups visiting together. This can present many challenges in acute care settings, and medical staff are sometimes frustrated by this, but it is an important factor in providing proper spiritual care to both the patient and their family.

Teaching on euthanasia[12] and suicide

In both religions, euthanasia and suicide are in general frowned upon. In Hindu teaching, the body is seen as the temple of the soul, and premature termination of life is a violation against natural law.[13] In Islam the body is viewed as belonging to Allah.

In a Hadith it is recorded *"Allah may forgive every son except in the case of one who dies mushrik or one who kills a believer intentionally."*[14] Islam does not regard euthanasia as justifiable. Surah 17:33 states *"You shall not kill any man whom God has forbidden you to kill, except for a just cause"*. It is Allah's decision alone when a person is to die; no one can add or subtract an hour from it.[15]

In practical terms if a Muslim becomes ill they ought to seek medical care. It is highly unusual for a Muslim patient to place a 'do not resuscitate order' on their notes. It is viewed as not doing everything possible to sustain life. Nonetheless, the prolonging of life by artificial means is also not encouraged.[16]

---

[12] For the purpose of this paper I will use the legal definition: "the intentional termination of life by another at the explicit request of the person who wishes to die."

[13] D. Thakrar and V. Aery, 'Death and Bereavement', in D. Thakrar (ed.), *Caring for Hindu Patients*, Oxford: Radcliff Publishing, 2008, p77.

[14] Reported by Abu Daoud, Ibn Hibban, and al-Hakim.
http://web.youngmuslims.ca/online_library/books/the_lawful_and_prohibition_in_islam/ch4s4p11.htm, cited 2nd June, 2011.

[15] Q.16:61.

[16] In Islam it is prohibited to not provide nourishment and hydration to the dying person (Salman, 'Considering Faith', p162). There have also been a number of fatwas issued by Saudi Arabia's Grand Mufti Shaikh Abdul Aziz bin Abdullah bin Baz stating that euthanasia is

Islam also prohibits suicide. In one Hadith,[17]

> "The Prophet said, "He who commits suicide by throttling shall keep on throttling himself in the Hell Fire (forever) and he who commits suicide by stabbing himself shall keep on stabbing himself in the Hell-Fire."

In another Hadith[18]

> "A man was inflicted with wounds and he committed suicide, and so Allah said: My slave has caused death on himself hurriedly, so I forbid Paradise for him." It needs to be noted, however, that nowhere in the Qur'an is suicide directly prohibited.

As with many issues, opinions about euthanasia vary within Hinduism. *Dharma*, the guiding principle for Hinduism, is open to wide interpretation, especially in terms of the duty to care for older members of one's family or community.[19] Euthanasia disrupts the timing of death and rebirth and yields bad *karma*. Because life is sacred, euthanasia is seen as not alleviating suffering but actually exacerbating it, in this life and the next.[20] This generates bad *karma* for the killed soul but also for the person doing the killing because of the violation of the principle of non-violence (*ahisma*).[21] On the other hand, when a doctor alleviates a person's suffering it is a good deed and fulfills moral obligations.[22] Patients themselves may seek an early death to ensure lucidity so they can pursue the ultimate goal of liberation from the material world.[23]

Suicide in Hinduism is not seen in terms of right or wrong but rather in terms of *karmic* impact. Suicide is seen as creating bad

---

un-Islamic and that it is against Shari'a to decide the death of a person before he is actually dead.

F. Zahedi, K. Aramesh and H. Shadi, 'Euthanasia: an Islamic Ethical perspective', *Iranian Journal of Allergy, Asthma and Immunology*, vol.6 Suppl., 5 February 2007, p36.

[17] Bukhari 2:23:446, narrated by Abu Huraira.

[18] Bukhari 2:23:445, Jundab narrated.

[19] Thrane, p56.

[20] Thakrar, p78. In Hinduism unlike in Islam the refusal of food and hydration is permitted.

[21] Nimbalker, p56.

[22] Nimbalkar, p56.

[23] Nimbalkar, p57.

karma, because it disrupts that natural cycle of death and rebirth. According to Gyan Rajhans:

> According to Hindu beliefs, if a person commits suicide, he neither goes to the hell nor the heaven, but remains in the earth consciousness as a bad spirit and wanders aimlessly till he completes his actual and allotted life time. Thereafter he goes to hell and suffers more severely. In the end he returns to the earth again to complete his previous karma and start from there once again. Suicide puts an individual's spiritual clock in reverse.[24]

An exception to this rule is *Prayopavesa,* or fasting to death. It is only acceptable in certain circumstances, such as when the body has served its purpose and it is the right time for life to end. As starving is a gradual process it allows the person time to reflect and prepare for death. Thus it originates not from despair, but from spiritual concerns.

The dying process

Both religions attach significance to the process of dying. To Hindus it can be an opportunity to learn new *karmic* lessons and move closer to *moksha*. The ideal for Hindus would be to die in old age, at the right astrological time and the right place. Hindus would prefer to die at home on the ground, so they are closer to mother earth.

For Muslims, death is also an important process. It brings one closer to meeting one's creator and also presents the opportunity to ask for Allah's forgiveness for sins committed. Again it provides the opportunity to submit to the will of Allah. There are a number of passages that Muslims can take encouragement from as death approaches:

> *As for those who say: "Our Lord is God" and take the straight path to Him — the angels will descend to them saying, "Have no fear and do not grieve. Rejoice in the Paradise you have been promised."Q 41:30*

---

[24] G. Rajhans, http://gyansrajhans.blogspot.com/2010/02/modern-hindu-views-of-suicide-and.html, cited 9th June, 2011.

Muslims believe in resurrection and final judgement. The Qur'an teaches *"The angel of death, who is given charge of you, shall cause you to die, then to your Lord you will be returned."* Q 32:11[25]

Death rites

In both religions the deceased needs to be treated with respect. There are many similarities between Hinduism and Islam on how the body is treated at death. For example, it is preferred that persons of the same gender as the deceased handle the body. For some Hindus this goes even further, in that some prefer that only Hindus handle the body.

The Muslim family, like any family, expects the deceased's body to be treated with dignity. Once death is formally pronounced, the rites of washing with scented water and shrouding in a seamless white cloth need to take place. The deceased will then be transported to the site of the funeral prayers, led by an Imam. The deceased is then taken to the cemetery for burial. They are laid in the grave on their right side facing Mecca. It is preferred that burial takes place within twenty-four hours of death. In Islam cremation is prohibited.

In Hinduism, when death is imminent the family needs to be called as well as a *Brahmin* (priest) who can pray with the family. The *puja* (last rites) may be performed by either a priest or the family. In the case of a father it is the eldest son and in the mother's case it is the youngest son. Most desire that drops of Ganges River water be placed in their mouths and leaves from the sacred *Tulsi* (basil) plant be placed on their bodies. Another tradition is that gifts for the poor be touched by the dying person to symbolise their generosity. The priest will tie a piece of sacred thread around the neck or wrist of the dying person. As in Islam, there is a ritual washing of the body.[26]

Unlike Islam, cremation is the traditional method of dealing with the body in Hinduism. It is viewed as the way to allow a swifter

---

[25] Zahedi et al., p10.

[26] D. Jootun 'Nursing with Dignity:.part 7 Hinduism ' *Nursing Times,* vol 98, issue 15, in http://www.nursingtimes.net, cited on 18th April, 2011.

release of the soul from the body. As in Islam, preference is for the body to be put to rest the same day.

The funeral itself has an important role to play in both Hinduism and Islam. In Hinduism there is to some extent a belief that the soul needs to be told that they have died. Those who are at the funeral provide guidance. In Hinduism, some funeral chants address the dead encouraging them to let go of their attachments to material things and continue their journey to their new existence.

In Islam following the funeral service, the family will remain[27] and make intercession for the deceased because of the belief they are being questioned by angels. One of the Hadith reads,

> *"When the Prophet, may Allah bless him and grant him peace, finished burying a dead person, he used to stand over him and say, 'Ask forgiveness for your brother and ask for steadfastness for him. Now he is being questioned.'"* [28]

Views on life after death

In both Hinduism and Islam there is a belief that all people have a soul. In Islam the Qur'an teaches the continued existence of the soul into eternity and that there is a transformed physical existence after death. This differs significantly from the Hindu teaching of reincarnation. In Hinduism the *atman* (soul) will go through infinite succession and permutation, passing many lives and experiences before merging with the divine.

For Muslims their eternal future depends primarily on performing good deeds, especially the keeping of the five pillars. The Qur'an explains that Allah will judge Muslims according to their deeds:

> *"Those whose good deeds weigh heavy in the scales shall triumph, but those whose deeds are light shall forfeit their souls and abide in hell forever."* (Q 23.102) [29]

---

[27] In Pakistan only the men go to the burial. The women go later to weep.

[28] Abu 'Amr, and it is said Abu 'Abdullah or Abu Layla, 'Uthman ibn 'Affan said, [Abu Dawud], extracted from http://www.sunnipath.com/library/Hadith/H0004P0161.aspx, cited 9th June, 2011.

[29] Ed: The following article discusses the different understandings of the afterlife in Hinduism and Islam in additional detail.

Islamic teaching on final judgement resembles that taught in Christianity. There will be a last trumpet, the dead will rise and everyone will be for paradise or hell.

There are Hadith accounts that speak about a place called *al-barzakh*. This is the interval between death and the resurrection. It is seen in terms of 'soul sleep', where there is no sense of time and there is also no means of communicating with the dead. Within this realm there are two states. One is the place of blessing and bounties of Allah due to one's faith and good deeds. The other is a realm of punishment. At death the deceased is questioned by two angels. The answers given determine whether the experience of the grave is pleasant or unpleasant for each person. The questions asked are, "Who is your God?", "Who is your prophet?" and "What is your faith?"[30]

For Hindus, one's hope is for a better rebirth, as the attaining of *moksha* is seen as almost impossible, although it is promised by Krishna in the *Gita*. The Hindu view on the judgement of a person's soul has certain similarities with that in Islam. The *Kaushitaki Upanishad* (1.2-6) explains it in this way;

> "the souls of the dead ascend to the moon which is the door of heaven; there they are questioned as to their identity and if they give a wrong answer, that is, if they fail to realize their identity with Brahman, they are condemned to further empirical existence in human, animal, bird, fish or reptile form 'according to their Karma, according to their knowledge.'[31]

The deeds of a person's life will influence whether one's soul continues to the cycle of rebirth or becomes one with Brahman.

Both Muslims and Hindus are reluctant to conduct autopsies. In Islam the body is sacred whether dead or alive. Thus cutting, mutilating or tampering with it in any way is considered *haram*.[32] This is because the soul remains in the body for a period following

---

[30] Amanda Parker, "Torment in the Grave and a Christian Response" in B.J. Neely & P.G. Riddell (eds.), *Islam and the Last Day: Christian Perspectives on Islamic Eschatology*, Melbourne: MST Press, 2014, p11-17.

[31] R.C. Zahner, *Hinduism*, Oxford: Oxford University Press, 1962, p60.

[32] The following hadith explains this. *The Messenger of Allah said: "Breaking the bone of a dead person is similar (in sin) to breaking the bone of a living person". (Sunan Abu Dawud, Sunan Ibn Majah & Musnad Ahmad)*

death. A second factor is the desire that in Hinduism the body be cremated and in Islam the body be buried as soon as possible following death.

Conclusion

Although Islam and Hinduism differ greatly in worldview when it comes to death there are many similarities. These include care for the dying and respect for the deceased. That there is more to life is apparent in both Hinduism and Islam. Both also hold that the essence of a person is not just flesh and bones, but rather a person's soul, which exists beyond death.

Islam is a monotheistic religion and Hinduism is polytheistic, so they have very different perspectives on the nature of the divine and eternity. Yet both have some strikingly similar views on judgement and the determination of a person's future particularly in relation to being questioned shortly after death.

As Western societies are changing rapidly consideration needs to be given to religious beliefs in the provision of end of life care. This presents many challenges. However, improved understanding of these needs will contribute to better holistic care practice.

THE AFTERLIFE IN HINDUISM AND ISLAM

Ee Ling Ting[1]

Introduction

Both Hinduism and Islam are deeply rooted within the South and East Asian regions. "Afterlife" is a subject of considerable discussion amongst scholars of both religions. Whilst Hinduism teaches reincarnation and *karma,* for Muslims, death represents the termination of physical life and the commencement of the 'rest' period in the grave, awaiting the Day of Resurrection upon which Allah will judge the living and the dead.[2]

The concept of afterlife in Hinduism

The concept of afterlife in Hinduism is based on *Samsara*: the wheel of birth, death, rebirth and reincarnation or the transmigration of the soul. According to the doctrine of reincarnation in Hinduism, there are divine consequences for every individual's behaviour (*karma*). The noun *karma* signifies cause and effect and originates from the root "kṛ", which means "to do, act, make, perform or accomplish". The idea of *karma* harks back to the Vedic *Brahmana* texts, where much significance is attached to the ritualistic and rite-driven deeds performed during the lifetime. Supposedly, our immortal essence (*jiva*) does not die with the body but reaps joy or suffering (*duhkha*) in proportion to one's acts. It is *karma* that, irrespective of one's status, caste and good intentions, decides one's fortune after death. Therefore, a person's behaviour determines what form he will take in the next life. Thus, Hindus are

---

[1] Ee Ling Ting originates from Malaysia. She completed a Master of Arts in Ministry at MST in 2012.

[2] Herbert Ellinger, *Hinduism*, London: SCM Press Ltd, 1995, pp4-7; K. Williams, 'Near-Death Experiences of Muslims', http://www.near-death.com/muslim.html, cited 5 July 2015; Patrick Sookhdeo, *Faith, Power and Territory: A Handbook of British Islam*, McLean, VA: Isaac Publishing, 2008, p15; F. E. Peters, *A Reader On Classical Islam*, Princeton: Princeton University Press, 1994, pp388-392.

shaped by *karma*, which affects their life now as well as their next life.[3]

Although most Hindus view life on earth as being painful, as every human is trapped on the wheel of reincarnation (s*amsara*), they regard reincarnation as a chance at obtaining a better status in life or at achieving true liberation and oneness with the divine (*moksha*). The *Brihadaranyaka Upanishad* 4:4:3 describes the doctrine of rebirth in the following terms:

> *"As a Caterpillar which has wriggled to the top of a blade of grass draws itself over to a new blade, so does the soul, after it has put aside its body draws itself over to a new existence."*

Similarly it is also mentioned by Krishna in the *Bhagavad Gita* 2:22:

> *"As a person puts on new garments, giving up old ones, the soul similarly accepts new material bodies, giving up the old and useless."*

Hence, in order to increase their chances of a better life after reincarnation, many Hindus look to personal effort to perform their duty. The ultimate aim of a Hindu is to achieve the coveted state of 'no *karma*'. They believe that once this state is achieved, a person will no longer have to suffer through the cycle of birth-rebirth. 'No *karma*' means that a person has achieved a state of *moksha*. A person in this state is considered to have achieved full awareness of the truth as written in *Upanishads* texts. In addition, Hindus believe that there is no judgment after death and by achieving, one achieves 'salvation' by becoming one with Brahman.[4]

[3]John Ankerberg & John Weldon, *The Facts on Hinduism*, Hong Kong: Tien Dao Publishing House Ltd, 2000, p57; Cybelle Shattuck, *Hinduism*, London: Routledge, 1999, pp41-47; Purusottama Bilimoria, *The Self and its Destiny in Hinduism*, Melbourne: Deakin University, 1990, pp30-37; David Burnett, *The Spirit of Hinduism*, Turnbridge Wells: Monarch Publications, 1992, pp71-85; Hillary Rodrigues, *Introducing Hinduism*, New York and London: Routledge, 2006, pp50-51; Gavin Flood, *An Introduction to Hinduism*, Cambridge: Cambridge University Press,1996, pp85-86;
Author Unknown, *The Concept of Life After Death In Hinduism and In Islam*, http://www.islamandhinduism.com/ih/Life%20after%20death.html, cited14 June, 2011

[4]Ankerberg, pp41-47; Bilimoria, pp30-37; R. C. Zaehner, *Hinduism*, Oxford University Press, pp58-79; Rodrigues, pp52-53; *The Concept of Life After Death In Hinduism and In Islam;* Chintamani Rath, *Yama: Basic Human Values in Hinduism- Reincarnation and Karma*, http://www.religioustolerance.org/rath01b.html, cited 20 June, 2011.

The *Bhagavad Gita* teaches the various paths of *yoga* that aid in understanding the true nature of the universe; an understanding that leads to liberation. There are three main *yoga* emphasized in the Hindu sacred texts:

(1) *jnana-yoga: jnana* in Sanskrit means "knowledge", "wisdom" or "discernment". *Jnana-yoga* is the "path of wisdom" and *jnana* meditation is many-faceted. It is a tool for understanding and transcending the human mind.
(2) *karma-yoga*: this refers to action and includes all acts committed by an individual from birth to death. *Karma* encompasses the idea of 'doing no harm and acting in accordance with the law of *dharma*. Therefore, *karma-yoga* is the path of 'doing' without concern of results, that is, without letting the result influence the act.
(3) *bhakti-yoga:* pure spiritual devotion is based on the doctrine of "Love is God and God is love". Everything is meaningless and no longer important in *bhakti yoga*. Krishna taught that *bhakti yoga* is the most direct method of experiencing liberation. The essence of *bhakti yoga* is that everything, be it the knower and knowledge, subject and object, deity and devotee, all become One.[5]

Paradise in the Hindu texts
Hindu cosmology proposes that above the earthly plane there are six heavenly planes: Bhuva Loka; Swarga Loka (meaning Good Kingdom, a heavenly paradise of pleasure, where a majority of the Hindu gods (*deva*) reside, including *Indra,* and beatified mortals; Mahar Loka; Jana Loka; Tapa Loka; and Satya Loka.[6]

---

[5] Shattuck, pp53-54; Rodrigues, pp158-165; Satguru Sivaya Subramuniyaswami, *Dancing with Siva, Hinduism's Contemporary Catechism*, Hawai'i: Himalayan Academy, 1993, p101; Author Unknown, *Jnana Yoga: The Yoga of Knowledge*,
http://www.self-realization.com/articles/yoga/jnana_yoga.html, cited 13 June, 2011;
Author Unknown, *Jnana Yoga*, http://www.yogaworld.org/jnana.html, cited 13 June, 2011;
Author Unknown, *Karma Yoga: The Path of Karma yoga means selfless service*,
http://www.sanatansociety.org/yoga_and_meditation/karma_yoga.html, cited 13 June, 2011.
Author Unknown, *The path of Bhakti Yoga: pure spiritual devotion is Bhakti Yoga*,
http://www.sanatansociety.orgyoga_and_meditation/bhakti_yoga.html, cited 13 June, 2011;
[6] Norman C. McClelland, *Encyclopedia of Reincarnation and Karma*, Jefferson NC: McFarland & Co Inc., 2010, p263.

In the Vedic texts, there are verses that mention "Paradise". For example, the fourth Vedic text, *Atharva Veda*, states at 4:34:2:

> *"Boneless, purified, cleansed with the purifier, bright (cuci), they go to a bright world; Jatavedas burns not away their virile member; in the heavenly (svarga) world much women-folk is theirs."* [7]

Furthermore, in the *Atharva Veda* 2:34:5 it is written:

> *"Foreknowing, let them first (purva) receive the breath (prana) coming to [them] forth from the limbs. Go to heaven; stand firm with thy bodies; go to paradise (svarga) by god-travelled roads".* [8]

In another reference, *Atharva Veda* says (4:34:6):

> *Having pools of ghee, having slopes of honey, having strong drink (sura) for water, filled with milk (ksira), with water, with curds ...* [9]

While in the *Rig Veda* 10:95:18 it is written:

> *O Aila, the loud-sounding clouds, these divines say to you, since you are indeed subject to death, let your progeny propitiate your revered cosmic forces with oblations, then alone you shall rejoice (with me) in heaven.* [10]

Hell

Hell is also described in the Vedas and referred to in the Sanskrit as *narakasthanam*.

> *"May the bounteous fire divine, consume them with his fiercely glowing sharp jaws like flames, who disregard the commandments and steadfast laws of most venerable and sagacious Lord."* (*Rig Veda* 4:5:4)

For Hindus, hell represents the place where the most sinful individuals are punished. However, Hindus believe that there is no Satan in hell and that it is not the final dwelling place of the soul. To

---

[7] W.Whitney, *Atharva Veda Samhita*, Harvard University Press, 1905, p78.
[8] Whitney, p206.
[9] *The Concept Of Life After Death In Hinduism And In Islam*
[10] *The Concept Of Life After Death In Hinduism And In Islam*

them, hell is considered an intermediate place, similar to purgatory, in which sinful souls experience suffering or punishment for a limited time. After the time is 'served', even the most evil of people are released from hell to once again enter the cycle of reincarnation.[11]

The concept of afterlife in Islam

Afterlife is a significant theme in Islam and the Qur'an. A fundamental tenet lies in the belief of resurrection and the final judgment (*al-qiyamah*), which is one of the six articles of faith. Following death, Islam teaches that the soul (spirit) is separated from the physical body and remains in a kind of "soul sleep", awaiting bodily resurrection on the day of Judgment. The archangel will blow a horn sending out a 'blast of truth'. Traditions say that Muhammad will be the first to be resurrected, and the Qur'an emphasises that no one can be spared from Judgment:

> "*Every soul shall have a test of death. And only on the Day of Judgment shall you be paid your full recompense. Only he who is saved far from the fire and admitted to the Garden will have attained the object (of life). For the life of this world is but goods and chattels of deception*"(Q 3:185).

Allah will judge all humans and creatures according to their deeds and faith. The Qur'an emphasizes the importance of being accountable for one's thoughts, words and deeds. Muslims are taught that a complete record is kept of each person's deeds and statements and that Allah will use this as reference on the Day of Reckoning, which is described in the Qur'an as a momentous event. The Qur'an also clearly describes how Allah will dispense his justice, and reiterates that all human beings will be questioned about their earthly life. In a conclusive act, Allah will send the wicked to hell and the good to paradise (Q 56:5-12; 84:1-12).[12]

---

[11] Satguru Sivaya Subramuniyaswami, p155; *Concept of Life after death in Hinduism and Islam;*
Victor J Zammit, *A Lawyer Presents the Case for Afterlife,*
http//www.victorzammit.com/articles/religions3.html, cited 20 June, 2011
[12] Sookhdeo, p15; F. E. Peters, p388-392; Abdullah Saeed, *The Qur'an - An Introduction*, New York and London: Routledge, 2008, p72; Oliver Leaman, *A Brief Introduction To Islamic Philosophy*, Cambridge: Polity Press, 1999, pp36-39; C.T.R. Hewer, *The First Ten Steps*, London: SCM Press, 2006, p85.

The Qur'an repeatedly affirms the notion of life after death, emphasising that this worldly life is both short and temporary. Allah teaches his followers that: "Indeed, the afterlife is better and longer lasting" (Q 42:36). Therefore, Muslims should not allow temporal things to distract them from devotion to Allah, and should serve Him, do good deeds, participate in charity and lead an ethical and moral life. In doing so they will please Allah and gain entrance into eternal paradise. There are also many passages in the Qur'an and Hadith that vividly describe the scene on Judgment Day; detailed to encourage Muslims in their faith.[13]

Paradise

In Islam, the words heaven and paradise (*al-jannah*) are used to describe the place where souls of the faithful dwell after judgment. Yet, many Muslims understand this metaphorically, basing their understanding on the Prophet's words, "(what is in Paradise is) what an eye has not seen, an ear has not heard, and which has not been imagined by the heart."[14]

In Arabic, the word *jannah* means "garden". The Qur'an describes it as being full of comfort and luxury with rivers of milk and purified honey. It abounds in all types of fruits. Here, no one is ever fatigued and neither is there any idle talk. There are no troubles, anxieties, sins, sadness or hardship in Paradise but instead, eternal peace and bliss. The Qur'an says:

> *"And reward them, for their steadfastness, with a Garden and silken robes. They will sit on couches, feeling neither scorching heat nor biting cold, with shady [branches] spread above them and clusters of fruit hanging close at hand. They will be served with silver plates and gleaming silver goblets according to their fancy, and they will be given a drink infused with ginger from a spring called salsabil. Everlasting youths will attend them – if you could see them, you would think they were scattered pearls – and if you were to look around, you would see bliss and great wealth: they will wear garments of green silk and brocade; they*

---

[13] Sookhdeo, pp388-392; Muhammad Khalid Masid, 'Death And The World of Imagination, Ibn al-Arabi's Eschatology', *The Muslim World*, vol.78, Jan 1988, p59-65; B. A. Robinson, *Introduction To Islam: Part 1- Its Origin, Muhammad, Texts, Beliefs, etc* http://www.religioustolerance.org/isl_intr.html, cited 20 June, 2011.
[14] Hadith Qudsi 37. Cf. 1 Corinthians 2:9.

will be adorned with silver bracelets; their Lord will give them a pure drink". (76:12-22)

And further:

"As to the Righteous, they will be in the midst of Gardens and Springs, taking joy in the things which their Lord gives them, because, before then, they lived a good life. They were in the habit of sleeping but little by night, and in the hours of early dawn, they (were found) praying for forgiveness; and in their wealth and possessions (was remembered) the right of the (needy), Him who asked, and him who (for some reason) was prevented (from asking)". (Q 51:15-19)

In Paradise, unclean bodily functions, along with illness, will be nonexistent. Body odour will be that of musk. Gold and silver will abound. One of the main functions of paradise will be spending time glorifying Allah.[15]

A favourite expression among Muslims is *in sha' Allah*: "if Allah wills". Muslims believe that in order to enter Paradise and receive their rewards they need to do everything within their power to please Allah. Qur'an 67:2 mentions:

"He who Created Death and Life, that He may try which of you is best in deed; And He is the exalted in Might, oft-forgiving."

Islam teaches that life on earth is a constant battle and should be seen as a test which, if passed, will lead to heavenly rewards. In order to achieve their heavenly rewards and maintain their faith, Muslims are directed to observe the five basic practices (Five Pillars of Islam). Of these the ritual prayer cycle (salat), the month of fasting (sawm), helping the poor (zakat) are mandatory. It is believed that observing these disciplines will lead to a stronger faith and help gain entrance into Paradise. Islam teaches that Satan is always seeking to tempt and lure Muslims away from their faith and obedience to Allah.[16] If that happens, life will be filled with suffering and difficulties. In the midst of this daily battle, Islam introduces a hope for the future, promising eternal reward for

---

[15] Phil Parshall, *Understanding Muslim Teachings And Traditions*, Grand Rapids, MI: Baker Book House Co., 1994, pp145-146.

[16] Ed. See Peter Riddell's article, 'Demonic Temptation in Buddhism and Islam' in this present volume.

those who are able to maintain their faith throughout struggle. However, for those who do not follow the commandments of Allah, or fail to maintain their daily discipline, the outcome is Hell.[17]

As Muslims believe in the existence of Allah, they therefore acknowledge his character. The ninety-nine names of Allah reveal his character, and devout Muslims believe that in reciting Allah's ninety-nine names without mistake, it shows not only their piety but gains entry to Paradise.[18]

Muslims can also enter Paradise through *jihad,* which is sometimes referred to as the sixth Pillar of Islam. *Jihad* is an Arabic word that means 'struggle' and is used in Islam to mean 'striving in the way of Allah'. It refers to both the inner struggle that one faces against sin, as well as the outer struggle against those who oppose Islam. Paradise is promised assuredly to those who die "in the way of Allah", struggling for Allah and fighting for the establishment of an Islamic society (*jihad*), as the following verses show.

> "*Allah did indeed fulfil His promise to you when ye with His permission were about to annihilate your enemy – until ye flinched and fell to disputing about the order, and disobeyed it.*" Q3:152

> "*Be not like the Unbelievers, who say of their brethren, when they are travelling through the earth or engaged in fighting: 'If they had stayed with us, they would not have died or been slain'*"Q3:156

> "*Think not of those who are slain in Allah's way as dead. Nay, they live, finding their sustenance in the Presence of their Lord; They rejoice in the bounty provided by Allah.*"[19] Q3:169

---

[17] Parshall, pp145-146; Abdullah Saeed, p73.

[18] Parshall, pp145-146; Muhammad Hamidullah, *Introduction to Islam*, London: MWH London Publishers, 1979, pp52-54; George W. Braswell, *What You Need To Know About Islam and Muslims*, Nashville: Broadman and Holman Publishers, 2000, p31; *The Concept Of Life After Death In Hinduism and In Islam*.

[19] Abdullah Saeed, p72; Farid Esack, *The Qur'an- a short Introduction*, Oxford: Oneworld Publications, 2002, p 178; George Grant, *The Blood of The Moon,* Nashville: Thomas Nelson Publishers,2001, pp123-125; Michael Bonner, *Jihad In Islamic History*, Princeton and Oxford: Princeton University Press, 2006, pp1-4; Peter G. Riddell & Peter Cotterell, *Islam In Context: Past, Present and Future*, Grand Rapids, Michigan: Baker Academic, 2003, pp28-29

In addition, an authoritative Hadith records that in heaven, each man will have two wives.[20]   In another Hadith,[21] it speaks of seventy-two wives or *houris* for each husband. These *houris* are special beings or creations of God (especially) for the eternal enjoyment of Muslim men. These women or companions remain young and beautiful. However, throughout Islamic writings, there are no references to suggest that Muslim women will have a husband in Paradise (or even get to Paradise).[22]

Hell

For a Muslim, how one's life journey ends is extremely important. They consider one's last deeds as having eternal significance, as well as determining their eternal destination. This does not mean that earlier actions are disregarded, but rather, a greater emphasis is placed on how one finishes the journey. Muslims are taught that those who do evil or disobey Allah will definitely be sent to the Hell. The Qur'an and Hadith describe Hell as a place watched over by powerful angels and inhabited by those who did not acknowledge and believe in Allah during their lifetimes; who did not follow the path and teachings of the prophets; and who were tyrannical and unjust in their dealings. Moreover, Hell (*jahannam*) is seen as a place of torment, where evildoers experience dire punishment with agony, resulting from being scorched by hellfire, a fire whose fuel is men and stones (Q2:24). The texts describe a scene where skins, though burnt, are constantly renewed so as to constantly feel pain and torment. Along with other Qur'anic verses,[23] Q78:21-30 says:

> "*Hell lies in wait, a home for oppressors to stay in for a long, long time, where they will taste no coolness nor drink except one that is scalding and dark - a fitting requital, for they did not fear a reckoning, and they rejected our messages as lies. We have recorded everything in a record. 'Taste this: all you get from us is more torment'.*"

---

[20] *Sahih Muslim* 7:2834.

[21] *Jami' al-Tirmihi*, 3:20:1663.

[22] Mark Durie, *The Third Choice*, Melbourne: Deror Books, 2010, p47.
[23] Q 2:24; 4:56; 14:16, 17:22; 19-22; 35:36,37. See *The Concept Of Life After Death In Hinduism and In Islam*.

A relevant Hadith is narrated by Abu Huraira:[24]

> *Allah's Apostle said, "your (ordinary) fire is one of 70 parts of the (hell) first." Someone asked, "O, Allah's Apostle! This (ordinary) fire would have been sufficient (to torture the unbelievers)." Allah's Apostle said: "The (hell) Fire has 69 parts more than the ordinary (wordly) fire, each part is as hot as this (worldly) fire".*

In a range of Qur'anic passages — 2:39, 2:161-162; 2:257, 3:16, 5:10, 5:86 — it also mentions that those who do not convert to Islam will go to hell. This includes unbelievers, apostates and sinners, as well as the wretched Christians and Jews, who cling to their belief and continue to reject Muhammad and his teachings.

> *"The unbelievers of the People of the Book and the idolaters shall be in the Fire of Hell, therein dwelling forever; those are the worst of creatures".* Q 98:6

Nevertheless, some Muslims are more open, allowing the possibility of non-Muslims reaching heaven after a period of purification in purgatory.[25]

Tortures in Hell

The Qur'an and Hadith offer detailed descriptions of torture in *Jahannam*, as discussed above. They include the burning of the skin, only to be replaced to be burnt again; the wearing of garments of fire; the scalding of the skin and organs by boiling water; the burning of faces, lips and backs; the roasting of the body from sided to side; and the dragging of faces and bodies (bound in yokes) through boiling water and fire. The Hadith introduces punishments not found in the Qur'an. For example, *Sahih al-Bukhari* records Muhammad saying, "Most of the residents of the hell are women", representing those wives who were ungrateful to their husbands.[26] Even the least-suffering person in hell will have their brain boiling from standing on hot embers.[27] Those who have committed suicide will be tortured in this way on the Day of Resurrection and in hell.

---

[24] *Sahih Bukhari*, 4:54:487.

[25] Zammit.

[26] Parshall, pp145-146.

[27] Narrated An-Numan: I heard the Prophet saying, "The least punished person of the Hell Fire people on the Day of Resurrection, will be a man under whose arch of the feet a

Comparison of Afterlife between Hinduism and Islam

i.   Although the doctrines and teachings of afterlife in Hinduism and Islam are very different in key ways, a noticeable similarity occurs. Both Hinduism and Islam teach their followers that in order to experience a better afterlife (*samsara*) or to enter Paradise, one needs to do good deeds in this current life. Hinduism encourages Hindus to do charity for good *karma* in order to be reincarnated as better beings, resulting in privileges in the next life. Islam commands Muslims to practise the five pillars of Islam because on Judgement day, Allah will direct people to Hell or Paradise depending on individual beliefs and deeds in this life.

ii. The way Islam and Hinduism portray Hell is very similar. It is a place full of fire and suffering. However, Islam explains it in more detail and describes it as a place where the residents of hell are women, unbelievers, those who are not loyal to Allah and those who commit apostasy.

iii. Neither Hinduism nor Islam teach that Satan is in hell.

iv. Hinduism considers the soul as never dying, while the physical body does. Therefore, Hindus regard death as an exalted experience, considering that the cycle of life, death and afterlife provide the path to perfect oneness with Brahman. For Muslims, Paradise is the final destination and the promised reward from Allah. Death is just another of life's natural processes, which should not be feared.

Contrast:

i.   In Islam, this worldly life is considered to be a test given by Allah, designed to sift out those who are unfit for eternal life in Paradise. Hinduism believes that the reason one's soul is in this world is to find the Eternal Truth and to "be one with Brahman".

---

smouldering ember will be placed so that his brain will boil because of it", *Sahih Muslim,*1:414; Parshall, pp138-139.

ii. Hindus believe that the cycle of life does not end, and that believers will reincarnated. Consequently, a person's behaviour will determine how they are reincarnated in the next life. However, the ultimate aim of every Hindu is to achieve a state of 'no karma'. In contrast, Muslims believe in the Day of Resurrection and the last judgement. For Muslims, the body is separated from the spirit at death, and that one's faith and actions in this life will determine one's fate after death. They believe that there is a Day of Judgment where life on earth will end, and all humans will be judged, and everyone sent either to Paradise or to Hell.

iii. Entering Paradise (*al-jannah*) is an anticipated event for Muslims. They believe that they must do all within their power to please and serve Allah, and for some this includes going to war against those who oppose Allah to establish an Islamic society for Allah. They are taught that if they do Allah's will, they will be rewarded with the bountiful blessing of Paradise: where there is wine, gold, wonderful places and young virgins. On the other hand, Hindus have a more pessimistic view of life, and believe that no matter what they do, the God they choose to worship will not reward them. They believe that every human being is trapped on the wheel of reincarnation (*samsara*) and might only be liberated after a lengthy process of fulfilling duty and subsequent rebirth, which are beliefs without any guarantees.

iv. Muslims believe that Allah will judge people according to their faith and deeds and send people to eternal Hell or eternal Paradise. The concept of Hell and Heaven in Hinduism is very different from that of Islam. Hindus believe that both Paradise and Hell are but temporary residences for humans in the wheel of reincarnation. After this transitory state, the soul will reincarnate as human, animal or even plant.

v. According to the Islamic primary texts, immortal life in Heaven is a joyous experience. Those who reside there are clothed in costly apparel, enjoy sumptuous banquets and are able to lie on couches inlaid with gold or precious stones. Heaven's residents will be with their parents, wives, and children. *Swarga*, meaning Good Kingdom, is the common term for heaven in Hinduism, where the majority of the Hindu gods (*deva*) dwell, including the king of gods, Indra, and beatified mortals.

vi. For Hindus, the Sanskrit term *moksha* signifies liberation from the never-ending cycle of deaths and rebirths. For Muslims, there is no release from death or suffering, but rather, rewards in Paradise for good deeds or acts.

vii. For Hindus, reincarnation is constrictive whilst for Muslims, pleasing and serving Allah (in order to gain entry to Paradise) is a welcome duty.

viii. The Qur'an suggests that those who do not accept the Qur'an and Muhammad, those who commit apostasy and unbelievers will go to Hell. Some Muslims believe that non-Muslims can still enter heaven after a period of purification in the fires of purgatory. For Hindus, there is no mention of unbelievers or resulting consequences after death.

Conclusion

While the concept of the afterlife in both Hinduism and Islam has a long history and strong textual support, there are significant similarities and differences in their respective beliefs. Both faiths teach that since the soul is perpetual and does not perish, the death of the body is to be accepted without fear. However, this has not necessarily given their believers a sense of freedom or joy; the concepts of reincarnation (in Hinduism) and Judgment day (in Islam) are burdensome to many of their believers. These concepts can lead followers to a legalistic approach to life, fulfilling certain rules or principles in order to gain rewards (good *karma*), liberation (*moksha*) or entrance into *al-jannah*.

BUDDHISM EMERGES FROM ITS HINDU ROOTS:
Historical and doctrinal factors [1]

Elizabeth Greentree [2]

Introduction

The extent to which Hinduism and Buddhism are separated is difficult to define. Burnett notes that while Hindu thought is divided into different schools, at its most fundamental level these schools can be divided into groups that accept the authority of the *Vedas* and are seen as orthodox and those which do not but are accepted as heterodox, which includes Buddhism. [3] Ch'en agrees that while Buddhism is often seen as 'the great aberration from Indian tradition', it needs to be admitted that it did not entirely depart from its predecessor. [4] Both of these views consider Buddhism from its connection to Hinduism, and Hindus' acceptance of Buddhism. However, this present study suggests that the emergence of Buddhism from Hinduism must reflect at some level a dissatisfaction with Hinduism in either its doctrines or its relation to society. In order to understand and identify this dissatisfaction, it is necessary to trace the development of Hinduism to determine the context in which Hinduism arose, and how that context, Hinduism or both changed. Moreover, this study argues that the emergence of Buddhism should also be viewed in terms of Buddhist self-identification. As Hall argues, self-identity is created in two ways: through the acknowledgement of internal common traits as well as through definition by opposition to

---

[1] This article first appeared in the *CSIOF Occasional Papers*, Issue 1, 2009, pp37-47.

[2] Elizabeth Greentree initially completed her undergraduate studies in Classics and Archaeology, with a B.A. Hons from the University of Melbourne. She then moved across to study Theology through the Melbourne School of Theology (previously the Bible College of Victoria) and obtained an M.Div. She continued doing research specialising in Old Testament studies, and is currently working full time while developing a potential PhD thesis in theological methodology and education.

[3] David Burnett, *The Spirit of Hinduism*, Tunbridge Wells: Monarch, 1992, p176.

[4] Kenneth Ch'en, *Buddhism: The Light of the East,* New York: Barron's Educational Series, 1968, p1.

external views.[5] Thus, the emergence of Buddhism from Hinduism needs to be understood in terms of historical and doctrinal factors which allowed for Buddhist self-identification, such as the revelation of the Buddha, as well as those factors which acted as a counterpoint for definition through opposition.

Considering these points, this study will first outline the social, political and economic factors which resulted in widespread dissatisfaction with traditional Hinduism and supported the emergence of a new religion, possibly influencing how that religion developed. Next, this study will discuss the development of Hinduism as a religion up to the time of the Buddha, particularly focusing on doctrinal points which were creating tension within the society. This is evidenced by a new focus in writings in the *Upanishads* compared to the earlier Vedic texts and the growing number of sects. Finally, this study will look internally within the Buddhist writings for their self-identification. This study sees future developments of Buddhism after its initial period (such as the development of Mahayana forms and their subsequent spread to other Asian countries) as unrelated to the topic, and will thereforefocus mainly on the Theravadic tradition, using the Pali Canon as representative of the Buddhist sacred texts for this early period.

Socio-Political Context

While there is debate, most modern scholars suggest that the Buddha lived in north India sometime in the 5th century BC.[6] Historically, this was a period of expanding bureaucratic empires.[7] Between the 7th and 6th centuries BC in India, sixteen small states around the Ganges Valley were reduced to four larger ones, which in the next two hundred years (roughly 550-350 BC) were consolidated into the Magadha Empire.[8] Darian suggests that this

---

[5] J. Hall, *Ethnic Identity in Greek Antiquity*, Cambridge: Cambridge University Press, 1997, p47.

[6] For example see Paul Williams, 'Buddhism: A Historical Overview' in C. Partridge, (ed.), *The New Lion Handbook: The World's Religions*, 3rd edn. Oxford: Lion Hudson, 2005, p188 and David Burnett, *The Spirit of Buddhism*, 2nd edn., London: Monarch, 2003, p13.

[7] Jean C. Darian, 'Social and Economic Factors in the Rise of Buddhism,' *Sociological Analysis* 38/3, 1977, p226. While acknowledging the development, Burnett suggests viewing the result as 'city states' in comparison to Darian's 'empires'. Also Burnett, p11.

[8] Darian, p227.

process was a flow-on effect from the earlier introduction of iron technology which initially allowed for the jungles to be cleared, and by the 7th century had created a population influx through migration.[9] Subsequently, this process led to the accumulation of greater economic surplus which resulted in military expansion, and as Burnett notes 'new wealth for some resulted in new social problems for all.'[10] These developments also brought about social change, in that they generated 'pressure to change those ideologies that serve to legitimate the status quo.'[11] Similarly, economic changes from pastoral or small cultivator, self-sufficient villages to the development of 'free floating' economies resulted in infrastructure changes which gave greater importance to the *vaishya*, the merchant class. This is demonstrated by the fact that by Mauryan times (approx. 322-185BC), the *vaishya* had become the wealthiest of the three top castes. [12]

However, the Vedic regulations and particularly the strong importance placed upon the caste system were ill-suited to these changes.[13] For example, the *Apastamba* prohibited visiting inferior men and travelling to foreign countries,[14] which were severe limitations for a merchant. There developed what verged on hostility between the Hindu writings and the economic centres. The *Dharma Sutras* prohibited the recitation of the Vedas in cities,[15] and even stated that it was impossible for one who lived in a town 'whose body is covered with the dust, (raised) by others, and whose eyes and mouth are filled with it' to obtain salvation, even if he restrained himself.[16]

Buddhism, on the other hand, was much more open to the needs of the merchants, which resulted in the acceptance of Buddhism by many. This can be seen within a century in the Magadhan capital at

---

[9] A. K. Warder, 'On the Relationships between Early Buddhism and Other Contemporary Systems,' *Bulletin of the School of Oriental and African Studies* 18/1, 1956, p46.

[10] Burnett, p11.

[11] Darian, p227.

[12] Darian, p234.

[13] For a discussion on the development of the caste system and its nature at the time of the Buddha, see Ch'en, pp10-11.

[14] *Apastamba* i.11.32.18.

[15] *Gautama* xvi.45.

[16] *Baudhyayana* ii.3.6.33.

Rajagriaha, which had 36,000 merchants' houses that were evenly divided between the Buddhists and the Jains.[17] Unlike Hinduism with its strong dependence upon the caste system as a support for *dharma*, Buddhism helped to create a broader range of affiliations, transcending the familial, village and caste relationships.[18] Furthermore, Buddhism also did not have the same concepts of ritual pollution held by Hinduism, which conflicted with the necessities of trade. Thus, Buddhism gained the support of the *vaishyas*, which considering the *vaishyas'* rise to prominence and wealth, proved one of the determining features for the long-term acceptance and continuation of Buddhism.

Similar to the *vaishya*, the rulers of early empires had two basic needs which conflicted with traditional Hinduism. First, there was the need for large revenues to support the military, public works and administrative expenses. Second, they needed a system of government which prevented the accumulation of wealth and power in the hands of potential rival groups. Darian states that the rulers in India overcame these problems by introducing a policy which attempted to free various social and economic resources previously controlled by the *brahman* and *kshatriya*.[19] Hinduism, however, with its vested interest in the status quo, stood opposed to these aims. The *brahman* priestly class, with their costly sacrifices and discouragement of trading, 'threatened the development of a market-type economy.'[20]

Conversely, Buddhism appealed to rulers as it offered no class to compete for power.[21] Further, Buddhism was not opposed to the gathering of wealth which a ruler needed, seeing it as a result of virtue for those who did it honestly:

> '*He who is virtuous and intelligent shines like a fire on a hill. He gathers wealth like a bee its honey. While hurting no one, his riches mount higher and higher.*'[22]

---

[17] Darian, p227.

[18] Darian, p230.

[19] Darian, also, later notes that during this time none of the kings of the major northern empires were *kshatriyas*, though traditionally according to the Hindu religious texts, they were the ruling caste. p230.

[20] Darian, p230.

[21] Darian, p230.

[22] Digha Nikayai iii: 189.

Darian concludes that the rise of Buddhism in India can be linked to its 'eminent suitability in meeting the political, economic and social needs of rulers and merchants in expanding empires.'[23]

Finally, for those social groups and castes which found little hope in either Hinduism or the new social changes, Buddhism offered a rebirth in heaven for the laity, something not possible within Hinduism.[24] Thus, for all levels of society, Buddhism developed a practical attraction.

In his argument, Darian has presented a number of facts about the correlation between the expanding empire and the acceptance of Buddhism. While he is working backwards, this paper suggests it is reasonable to read forward as well: that the needs of the empire, which were not being met by Hinduism, influenced the development of Buddhism so that it could take advantage of the weakness of Hinduism in order to establish itself.

Religious Context: Tracing the rise of Hinduism

Ch'en argues that to fully understand the emergence of the Buddha and his teachings, it is necessary both to understand the religious and social background as well as the contemporary conditions.[25] This section will focus on tracing the beginning of Hinduism and the development of the religion up to the time of the Buddha.

Unlike Buddhism which can be traced to a foundational figure, Hinduism had no single historical founder and a lack of any centralized authority, which has resulted in a multitude of different beliefs and doctrines.[26] Hinduism appears to have antecedents as early as the Indus Valley civilization which was a highly developed urban culture between 2500-1500 BC.[27] Little is known about the

---

[23] Darian, p236.

[24] Warder, p45.

[25] Ch'en, p1.

[26] Maya Warrier, 'Hinduism: A Historical Overview', in C. Partridge (ed.), *The New Lion Handbook: The World's Religions,* 3rd edn., Oxford: Lion Hudson, 2005, p134.

[27] Its development can be ascertained from the nature of the city, with its sophisticated water distribution, drainage and garbage disposal technologies and well-developed systems of farming, grain-storage and pottery. See Warrier, p134.

religion of this period; however, terracotta figurines suggest a primitive form of some Hindu deities such as Shiva and the mother goddess.[28] This civilization rapidly declined in 1800-1700 BC, and in its place developed the Aryan culture, which created Hinduism as it is understood today.[29]

Knowledge of the early forms of this society come from the Vedas, early Sanskrit texts compiled over hundreds of years.[30] Warrier argues that the Vedic texts 'constitute the foundation of most later developments in Hinduism', which is supported by the fact that many Hindus today still regard the Vedas as revelations on the true nature of Hinduism.[31] Similarly, Burnett considers the Vedas as the test of orthodoxy within Hinduism.[32] However, the Vedic texts do not focus on matters of doctrine. For example, Kalupahana notes that there is no mention of the doctrine of rebirth, which becomes central to Hinduism in the later Vedic period.[33] Rather, the texts focus on the detail of rituals.

Ch'en argues that originally the rituals were probably simple ceremonies performed by the domestic hearth twice a day and for important events. At the time the purpose of the ritual was to invoke the favour of the gods upon the household.[34] However, as the culture developed, later rituals became more complex, with many altars and numerous priests. The *Rig Veda*, probably the earliest Veda, depicts the ritual as initiated by a wealthy sponsor (*yajamana*) and performed by ritual specialists.[35] The purpose of the rituals also became more complex. Rather than granting favour, Ch'en argues that the purpose was to 'compel or coerce the gods to

---

[28] Warrier, p134. This needs to be viewed cautiously, as many civilizations of this period used mother goddess figurines.

[29] Though, as Warrier points out, there is debate as to whether this culture developed out of the Indus Valley civilization, or whether it came externally through migration or conquest. Warrier, pp134-135.

[30] Warrier, p135.

[31] Warrier, p135.

[32] Burnett, p176.

[33] Though he does note that 'some hymns indicate belief that a righteous man would go to the realm of the gods to dwell in immortality.' David J. Kalupahana, *A History of Buddhist Philosophy,* Honolulu: University of Hawaii Press, 1992, p3.

[34] Ch'en, p3.

[35] Warrier, p135.

do what men wanted them to do.'[36] This change led to an increase in the prestige of the *brahman* priests as having mysterious powers capable of controlling the universe and the gods. Ch'en notes that the *brahman* became so powerful that through deliberately committing errors in the ceremonies, they could destroy their patrons.[37] So central were the *brahman* to Hinduism at this stage that many scholars prefer to refer to the religion as 'brahmanism', reflecting the importance of the priests and the more unified reading of the Vedic texts, than is the case with the inclusive and complex belief system of later Hinduism.[38]

From this earlier period until just before the time of the Buddha, this brahmanistic ideology was central to social and political life. Warrier notes its importance based upon its concern with 'the ritual status and duties of the king, the maintaining of social order and the regulation of individual behaviour in accordance with the all-encompassing ideology of duty or righteousness (*dharma*).'[39] So closely tied were religion and society that *dharma* was based upon correct conduct not only for your stage in life (*ashrama*) but also for your social class (*varna*).[40] There could be no religious righteousness for those who chose to be outside of society as it was constructed.

It was within this context of increased complexity and importance upon rituals, Ch'en argues, that the concept of *samsara* developed.[41] While this concept would continue to be important within Hinduism and Buddhism, it also brought the impetus for reaction. With the concept of the cyclical nature of time came the concept of *moksha*, or ultimate liberation, which could only be obtained through *dharma*.[42] The complex ritualism of the time denied

---

[36] Ch'en, p3.

[37] Ch'en, p3.

[38] For example Nath defines the difference as 'whereas Brahmanism had represented more or less a single religious strand drawing mainly upon Vedic ideology and throughout manifesting an elitist outlook Puranic Hinduism proved to be a multiplex belief-system which grew and expanded as it absorbed and synthesized polaristic religious ideas and cultic traditions.' Vijay Nath, 'From 'Brahmanism' to 'Hinduism': Negotiating the Myth of the Great Tradition' *Social Scientist* 29/3, 2001, p20.

[39] Warrier, pp135-137.

[40] Warrier, p137.

[41] Ch'en, p4.

[42] Tinu Ruparell, 'Hinduism: Philosophy' in C. Partridge, (ed.), *The New Lion Handbook: The World's Religions*, 3rd edn., Oxford: Lion Hudson, 2005, p141.

moksha to the majority of the population, which 'inevitably led to reaction.'[43]

The later Vedic period is characterised by the move away from complex sacrifices to an emphasis upon personal worship and an intimate relationship with a particular deity.[44] Through this *moksha* became, theoretically at least, accessible by the multitude.[45] Rather than a ritualistic focus, it became an intellectual movement where speculations became all important.[46] Thus, the development of the *Aranyakas*[47] and *Upanishads* demonstrated the growing resistance to ritualism and 'a preference for more contemplative and spiritual forms of worship.'[48] Warder suggests that a 'disillusionment in the benevolent monarchy must have contributed strongly' to the move towards philosophy and mysticism.[49]

Two important concepts came out of the speculation within the *Upanishads*: *Brahman* (the universal essence)[50] and *atman* (the soul). The conclusion was reached that the *atman* and the *brahman* must be the same thing,[51] reflected in the catch phrase *tat tvam asi* 'that art thou'.[52] Based upon this, the central knowledge which gurus sought was the understanding that all is one, and the unity of one's own experience with the universe.[53] At the time various schools of thought arose to teach means of achieving this correct understanding. During this period there were three main schools. First, *Samkya-Yoga*, which taught *moksha* as a return to the blissful state of pure spirit, achieved through yoga. Second, *Nyaya-Vasheshika* taught the necessity of logical reasoning and right

---

[43] Ch'en, p4.

[44] Warrier, p138.

[45] Ch'en, p4.

[46] The term 'upanishad' means 'to sit at the feet' suggesting receiving knowledge personally from a teacher, which Ch'en argues developed connotations of secret knowledge. Ch'en, p4

[47] Ed. *Aranyakas* are expositions of the *Veda* from approximately 8th century BC. the *Upanishads* date from about the 8th century onwards.

[48] Theodore Gabriel, 'Hinduism: Sacred Writings' in C. Partridge (ed.), *The New Lion Handbook: The World's Religions*, 3rd edn., Oxford: Lion Hudson, 2005, p144.

[49] Warder, p46.

[50] Ed. This should not be confused with the *brahman/brahmin* priestly class.

[51] Burnett, p12.

[52] Ch'en, p7.

[53] Ch'en, p6.

understanding of reality as the means to *moksha*. Finally the *Mimamsa-Vedanta* school was critical of the other two views and argued for the fulfilment of *dharmic* duty, which would result in the cessation of rebirth and realization of one's true relationship with *Brahman*.[54] Outside of these schools, many others sought methods of liberation, particularly through self-discipline and asceticism. These groups were known as *sramanas* or strivers, and relied upon self-mortification as the means to liberation. 'They tortured their bodies by taking as little food as possible, or they did not sit, or they sat on thorns'.[55] Burnett and Warrier argue that it was from among these groups that Buddhism arose.[56] However, the Buddha was not satisfied with either the ritualistic Brahmanism of the time nor the strict austerity of the various *sramanas* sects.

The Buddhist Identity

The term 'Buddhism' arose through identification with the historical figure Siddhartha Gautama, though 'Buddha' itself was used throughout Indian history as a title to refer to someone who had gained particular insight into reality or reached the highest level of consciousness.[57] This leads to the question of how important the actual person of the Buddha is in a study of the historical and doctrinal context from which the movement arose. Burnett argues that there can be no understanding of Buddhism without understanding the personality behind it.[58] Williams, however, argues that Buddhism itself has always been more interested in his teachings and how the life story illustrates Buddhist teachings, than in the historical figure.[59] This present study agrees with Williams that the figure of Buddha himself is not as important as his teachings. This is supported by the fact that the life story of the Buddha developed over centuries. Burnett argues that it probably even went through three stages of development: from biographical fragments to fuller accounts written in Sanskrit or Pali and finally many late biographies composed in local

---

[54] This final school is the only one still existing today. Ruparell, pp141-142.

[55] Ch'en, p7.

[56] Burnett, p12 and Warrier, p137.

[57] Burnett, p10.

[58] Burnett, p10.

[59] Williams, 'Buddhism: A Historical Overview', p188.

languages throughout Asia.[60] Having said that, some identification of the Buddha is important in this particular study as it determines the historical and social context within which Buddhism emerged.

Barnes outlines the generally accepted facts of the Buddha's life:

> At the age of 29, disgusted by the poverty and injustice he saw in his father's kingly capital of Kapilavastu and resentful of the traditional claims of contemporary priests, the brahmans, that 'the Vedas [texts] were the sole and infallible source of religious truth', he rejected his luxurious worldly ways for the life of an ascetic.[61]

This brief history summarises two important points of the Buddha's life. First was his realisation of the universality of suffering through poverty and injustice. This realisation became the basis of all his teaching, the essence of which is presented in his first sermon:

> '*Now this, bhikkhus, is the Noble Truth of Suffering; Birth is Suffering; Decay is Suffering, Disease is Suffering; Death is Suffering; association with those one does not love is Suffering; separation from those one loves is Suffering; not to get what one wants is Suffering; in short, the five constituent groups of existence which are the object of Clinging are Suffering.*'[62]

From this basis the Buddha concluded that the answer was the cessation of desires, 'the complete fading away and extinction of this craving, its forsaking and giving up, liberation and detachment from it.'[63] This cessation could only be achieved through the exercise of the Buddha's Noble Eightfold Path. Thus Buddhism was internally defined based upon the acceptance of this doctrine. However, the Buddha also externally defined Buddhism by what it was not:

> '*These two extremes, bhikkhus, are not to be practised by one who has gone forth from the world. What are the two? 1) that conjoined with the passions luxury, low, vulgar, common,*

---

[60] Burnett, p13.

[61] Gina L. Barnes, 'An Introduction to Buddhist Archaeology', *World Archaeology: Buddhists Archaeology* 27/2, 1995, p165. The quote is from Ch'en, p11.

[62] Part 1, from the *Dhammacakkapavatana Sutta, Mahavaggta Pali, Vinaya Pitaka,* trans. Kaba-Aye U Chit Tin, 1981, reproduced at http://www.nibbana.com/tipitaka/tipilist.htm.

[63] Part 3, from the *Dhammacakkapavatana Sutta, Mahavaggta Pali, Vinaya Pitaka.*

ignoble, and unprofitable, and 2) that conjoined with self-mortification painful, ignoble and unprofitable. There is a Middle Way, O! bhikkhus, avoiding these two extremes, discovered by the Tathagata, a path which opens the eyes and bestows understanding, which leads to peace of mind, to higher wisdom, to full Enlightenment, to Nibbana.' [64]

The Buddha had studied under two different gurus, before finding his own way to enlightenment. However, while he was with these two gurus, 'he became convinced that true enlightenment was not to be found within Brahmanism.[65] While little is written concerning the two gurus under which he studied, considering the two extremes the Buddha references in his first sermon, it would be reasonable to suggest that the first was a more traditional brahmanic sect, while the second could have been one of the wandering *sramanas* who practiced harsh asceticism. In his first sermon, the Buddha is defining his movement in opposition to both of these groups.

The Buddha obviously did not agree with the wealth, importance and ritualistic traditions of the *brahmans*. Poussin argues that this can be seen in the difference in the definition of *karma* between Hinduism and Buddhism. He sees Buddhism as stepping forward away from Hinduism in acknowledging morality as central to *karma*, rather than Hindu tradition which argued for ritual.[66] Ch'en also argues that the Buddha 'repudiated the brahmanical claims that the *Vedas* were the sole and infallible source of religious truth.'[67] In the *Discourse Concerning the Brahmin Janussoni*, the comparison is made between the ways of the *brahman* and the Buddha. Within the discourse, Ananda, a follower of the Buddha took his bowl in the morning to collect alms and saw the *brahman* Janussoni who was in an all-white carriage drawn by all white mares, fitted with all white decorations, draperies, reigns, driver's whip, umbrella, head-dress, dresses, sandals and even being fanned by white fans made of a yak's tail. The sight of the carriage caused all the people to exclaim that it was a vehicle of noble people. The Buddha, on hearing the account of this, refuted the saying of the

---

[64] The Beginning, from the *Dhammacakkapavatana Sutta, Mahavaggta Pali, Vinaya Pitaka.*

[65] Burnett, p17.

[66] L. de la Vallee Poussin, *The Way To Nirvana*, 1917, Reproduced at sacred-texts.com, pp73-74.

[67] Ch'en, p11.

people and turned Ananda towards the Right View: that it is the Teaching which is the vehicle of the noble.[68] This discourse demonstrates the Buddha's dislike for the show of the *brahman* and juxtaposes the poverty but wisdom of his followers to the riches but vanity of the *brahman*.

Based on the obvious dislike for the ritualism and power-craving nature of the *brahman*, some have argued that the teachings of the Buddha continued some of the revolution begun in the *Upanishads*.[69] Darian defines this Upanishadic period as a rejection of the 'role of the priests as the supreme spiritual authority, substituting instead, the ability of the individual to reach enlightenment through philosophic understanding.'[70] While in basic summary the Upanishadic period and the aims of Buddhism sound very similar, in actual doctrine they reach very different conclusions. As discussed above, the Upanishadic thought led to the conclusion that *atman* and *Brahman* are the same, and enlightenment is found through the realisation of the oneness of everything. Buddhist teaching, on the other hand, is not concerned with unity, but impermanency. As Harris argues, Buddhists do not believe 'that there is an unchanging soul to reincarnate, but rather an ever-changing process of cause and effect.'[71] Moreover, the Buddha was not interested in the endless speculation found in the *Upanishads*. Buddhism was always focused primarily on the doctrine of salvation, with an 'intensely practical attitude.' [72]

It seems more likely that initially, having dismissed the *brahmans*, the Buddha did in fact turn to the ascetics and the teachings that arose from a focus on the *Upanishads*, which constituted his second teacher. However, sects such as the Jain, which developed into a separate entity from Hinduism as Buddhism did, achieved liberation by negating the results of previous *karma* through severe

---

[68] *Janussoi Brahmana Sutta, AvijjaVagga, Magga Samyutta, Mahavagga Samyutta, Samyutta Nikaya, Suttanta Pitaka,* trans. U Ko Lay, 1998, reproduced at
http://www.nibbana.com/tipitaka/tipilist.htm.
[69] Darian, p235.
[70] Darian, p235.
[71] Elizabeth J. Harris, 'Buddhism: Beliefs' in C. Partridge, (ed.) *The New Lion Handbook: The World's Religions,* 3rd edn., Oxford: Lion Hudson, 2005, p203.
[72] Edward Conze, *Buddhism: Its Essence and Development*, New York: Harper Torch books, 1975, p15.

austerities such as self-denial, fasting and going unwashed.[73] The Buddha in his first sermon warns equally against such extremes of austerity, and his other writings refute the six major teachers at the time.[74] Considering this, it is unlikely he or his followers would have identified themselves as a continuation of this extreme ascetic doctrine.

Conclusion

The historical factor that most affected the emergence of Buddhism from Hinduism was the changing nature of society. This saw a development from smaller more traditional political units which sought to maintain power and the status quo through the Vedic traditions to expanding empires which were restricted by these traditions and came into conflict with them. Buddhism, however, adapted and better satisfied the political and economic needs of the merchants and rulers. 'This encouraged the adoption of Buddhism by the two social groups who served as the chief agents of change in the growing empires.'[75] Further, it offered hope to those who had previously been denied enlightenment or a positive view of the next life by traditional Brahmanism.

Two key doctrinal factors contributed to Buddha's emergence. First was both Buddha's belief in the impermanency of all things, which conflicted with current thoughts about enlightenment based upon the realisation of the unity of all things, and second the movement's desire to be differentiated from both the traditional brahmanistic and the newer ascetic views. The development of the Buddhist identity can be seen in terms of answers to the historical and doctrinal problems of the time as well as a rejection of other answers that had been put forward by Hinduism and other sects. While many scholars focus on the Hindus' acceptance of Buddhism, this paper has suggested that the emergence of Buddhism needs also to be understood in terms of Buddhism creating self-identification through both the collecting of common elements and through the rejection of many Hindu and ascetic doctrines and beliefs. While probably initially studying under a brahmanic guru

---

[73] Burnett, p12.

[74] Ch'en, p8.

[75] Darian, p226.

then one of the harsh ascetic gurus, the Buddha rejected both of these. Rather, Buddhism defined itself through the internal wisdom of the impermanency of everything, and the external rejection of both extremes.

THE INTERCONNECTION BETWEEN BUDDHISM AND CHINESE RELIGIONS

Anya Kutchen[1]

China has a long history of religious and philosophical expression and there have been many influences on the development of the variety of beliefs. Buddhism has had a significant impact on Chinese traditional religious thinking, but has also itself been shaped by Chinese religions. In this paper we will explore various elements of Chinese traditional religions, Confucianism and Taoism before the arrival of Buddhism, the arrival and development of Buddhism in China, and the influence Buddhism and traditional Chinese religions have had on each other.

China before Buddhism

Before Buddhism was introduced to China, beliefs and rituals regarding ancestors, gods, and natural forces were prevalent. Although there were commonalities, certain beliefs and customs varied between locations. An example of this is how heroes who, treasured over time, became venerated as gods with reference to a specific locality.[2] There were also commonalities between the religions in China before Buddhism arrived, such as a priority of prosperity for the family and community, respect and worship of ancestors and a cross-over of the physical and spiritual worlds.

Ancestors

For many centuries Chinese thinking has placed a strong emphasis on family. Perhaps related to this is the Chinese veneration of ancestors. A person must respect and honour their ancestors and

---

[1] Anya Kutchen is a graduate student at the Bible College of South Australia, and has worked among international students in Adelaide with the Australian Fellowship of Evangelical Students.

[2] D. L. Overmyer, *Religions of China : The World as a Living System,* Religious Traditions of the World; San Francisco: Harper, 1986, p23.

work hard to continue their ancestors' legacy.[3] There is also an understanding that the spiritual world has a large impact on the physical world, which adds incentive to worship ancestors, as they have the power to bless and to curse. A person's interaction with their ancestors through reverence and offerings affects the ancestor's decisions, which in turn influence the living person and their prosperity. It was believed that an ancestor could cause bad things to happen to the family if they were angry, for example if their grave was not cared for properly or they were not given sufficient offerings.[4]

Nature

Nature was considered to be very closely connected with people, especially as people heavily depended on agriculture, and it was believed that there were gods or spirits connected with different parts of nature. People could not overcome nature, but were at the mercy of inhospitable environments. Therefore, they needed to look to the gods and spirits to help. Offerings needed to be made to these gods or spirits so that they would show favour and bring prosperity to the people. Rituals at particular times of year were also required to maintain the balance of nature and cosmic forces. Kings especially were expected to perform certain rituals and rule in the right way. Consequently, natural disasters, wars and crop failures were often attributed to kings or officials doing something wrong, so they were required to repent and atone for their wrong-doing by offering sacrifices or doing additional good deeds.

The following is an example of a ritual required of a king: on the day of the winter solstice, when the force of *yin* (associated with cold and dark) was dominant, the king would sacrifice a red bull which was a symbol of *yang* (associated with heat and light). This would ensure that spring and warmth would return, and consequently affected the livelihood of the nation.[5] Although Taoism further developed the concepts of *yin* and *yang* and focused on the importance of maintaining their correct balance, these were

---

[3] Overmyer, p15.

[4] Overmyer, p27.

[5] Overmyer, pp26, 73.

already common ideas among most Chinese schools of thought.[6] *Feng-shui* is also related to the idea of spirits and forces in nature. *Feng-shui* is the practice of choosing sites for buildings or even tombs, and arranging structures or furniture within the buildings, so that they are harmonious with the landscape and natural forces, which will consequently allow a good flow of energy and bring good fortune.[7]

Gods, Spirits and Divination

In the Shang Dynasty (approximately 1800-1040BC), kings and priests were diviners on behalf of the people. They inquired of the spirits regarding weather, crops and military issues, and made offerings to the gods of nature for safety and prosperity. It was believed that, if the offerings and associated rituals were done correctly, the god or spirit was required to respond favourably.[8]

During the Zhou Period (1040-256BC) the idea of a high god, or God of Heaven (called *Tian* or *T'ien*), became prominent. The God of Heaven gave authority to kings, if they were just and compassionate, but also gave justification to others to either rebuke or remove the king if he was unjust.[9] Other gods were still present and important, but *Tian* ruled over all other gods as well as the world.

Also during the Zhou Period, however, there was growing scepticism about the power, and even the reality, of gods, ancestors and the Tian. The gods did not appear to be protecting the people from wars and natural disasters or prospering the people who did right. This led to the rise of philosophy and focus on humans more than spirits.

Confucianism

---

[6] W. Corduan, *Neighboring Faiths : A Christian Introduction to World Religions*, Chicago: Inter-Varsity Press, 1998, p282.

[7] Overmyer, p61.

[8] Overmyer, p25.

[9] Overmyer, p26.

While Confucianism is a philosophy rather than a religion, we will consider it alongside religions, due to its significant influence on Chinese thought both before the introduction of Buddhism and also in more modern times. Confucius lived between 551-479BC and developed a philosophy of morals to be adhered to by people of all stations in life, such as honesty, justice, love, empathy, compassion, ethical commitment, frugality, hard-work, and the aim to improve society.[10] These morals are to be displayed by respect for parents, loyalty to friends, and care for others. In essence, Confucian thought directs all people to act in ways appropriate to their positions and relationships: a father should act as a father, and a son should act appropriately for a son. If everyone acted properly, according to their position in society, society would be well-ordered and harmonious.[11]

Confucianism does not focus so much on propositional truth, but emphasises finding the right 'way' to live in the world, to lead to social harmony. Philosophy and ideas were only relevant or useful if they led to knowing how to act, so abstract thinking was not valued.[12] Confucius claimed that these morals were the "will of Heaven" and that Heaven (possibly referring to the God of Heaven, or *Tian*) had given him power and authority to teach; however, Confucius did not believe in spirits and divination.[13] The teaching of Confucius and his primary disciple Mencius became more popular during the Warring States era (403-221BC), when there was a longing for peace and prosperity under one good ruler. However they were only taken on at a state level during the Eastern Han dynasty (25-220AD).[14]

Taoism

The philosophy and religion of Taoism is attributed to the teachings of Lao-zi (or Lao-tzu), who lived in the 6th/5th century BC. His teachings are compiled in the *Tao-te-ching* ("book of the way

---

[10] Overmyer, p28.

[11] J. K. Fairbank, *China: A New History,* The Belknap Press of Harvard University, 1992, p52.

[12] R. E. Nisbett, *The Geography of Thought, How Asians and Westerners Think Differently...And Why*, USA: Free Press, 2003, p19.

[13] Corduan, p293. Overmyer, p28.

[14] Fairbank, p51.

and its power").[15] As mentioned earlier, *yin* and *yang* were already elements of Chinese thought. They are opposing, but complementary forces, which ideally remain balanced. The *Tao* (or *Dao*), is the 'way', and is the properly balanced state of *yin* and *yang*. Essentially, Taoism seeks balance of *yin* and *yang* in the world, but the means of achieving this is by non-interference and acceptance of the way things are. A person should not try to fix the balance, or even try to find the *Tao*, as it cannot be found by a person's effort. The *Tao* cannot even be described or understood through language; it must reveal itself.

Taoism is relativistic, because, due to the changing nature of life and the world, something may be true now, but not true later.[16] In fact it is not concerned with truth, but the 'way' to be in balance with nature.[17] It promotes a passive approach to life and acceptance of the way things are. A person cannot know what will happen; circumstances may be good now, but bad situations may arise later. The interaction of opposing forces is what makes up life and the world. This can be observed but cannot be controlled, so one must accept it and not try to interfere with it.

Some scholars emphasise that Taoist writings and oral traditions have strongly influenced popular religions.[18] Nesbitt also notes that Confucianism and Taoism integrate; however, an individual might hold more strongly to one system than the other, especially depending on their life situations. He states "...every Chinese is a Confucianist when he is successful and a Taoist when he is a failure."[19] Perhaps it is easy to uphold Confucian philosophy when successful, as it can be seen that Heaven has determined the individual will be successful. But if an individual is a 'failure', it is seen as a time of *yin* that will eventually be opposed by *yang*.

Buddhism

---

[15] Corduan, p286.

[16] Fairbank, p53.

[17] Nisbett, p16.

[18] R. J. Leamaster and A. Hu, "Popular Buddhists: The Relationship between Popular Religious Involvement and Buddhist Identity in Contemporary China," *Sociology of Religion* 75, no. 2 (2014), p238.

[19] Nisbett, p16.

Buddhism was developed by Indian prince, Siddhartha Gautama, who lived around 500BC. He was raised as a Hindu, but became concerned with the problem of suffering and how to find liberation from suffering, death and rebirth. He claimed to have attained enlightenment after a period of meditation, in which he understood that suffering is caused by desire, and therefore eliminating desires is the way to be liberated from suffering and the cycle of death and rebirth and ultimately achieve Nirvana. The Buddhist definition of Nirvana is understanding that the self does not exist, as most people understand it, but is the result of a chain of cause and effect, both physical and mental. If the self does not exist, all desires are in a way unnecessary and can be eliminated. The chain of cause and effect continues, whatever a person does, whether good or bad, and does not cease with death. A person's actions in one life create karma, or effects, both in this life and the next life. A person's good actions will create good effects in their next life, and bad actions in this life create bad effects in the next. However the aim of Buddhism is not so much to create good karma and so have a better life when reborn, but to actually escape from karma and rebirth altogether. An enlightened person is freed from the effects of karma, because they can live and act with complete detachment, and consequently they do not need to be reborn.

As he taught his findings to his disciples, Gautama became known as the Buddha, the Enlightened One. Gautama developed the Four Noble Truths and the Eightfold Path as the means to realising the "way things are" and achieving enlightenment. The Four Noble Truths are to first identify the existence of suffering, secondly to understand that desire causes suffering, and thirdly to overcome desire. The fourth truth is to follow the Eightfold Path, or eight habits, which can be grouped into the categories of wisdom, ethical conduct and mental discipline.[20]

There are two main branches of Buddhism. Theravada Buddhism is primarily what the Buddha taught, and is atheistic. Mahayana Buddhism is the other predominant branch and is generally what is practised in China. In Mahayana Buddhism, the Buddha has been

---

[20] J. Dickson, *A Spectator's Guide to World Religions: An Introduction to the Big Five,* Sydney, Australia: Blue Bottle Books, 2005, 52-73; M. Baumann, "Buddhism," in *Religions of the World: a comprehensive encyclopedia of beliefs and practices,* eds. J. Melton, et al.; Santa Barbara, California: ABC-CLIO, LLC, 2010, p181.

elevated to a god-like position, and is able to help Buddhists achieve enlightenment, when they give offerings at shrines and temples. Mahayana Buddhism also teaches that some people, called bodhisattvas, who have achieved enlightenment but have compassion on those who have not, may remain in the cycle of death and rebirth in order to teach and help others achieve enlightenment.[21] There are further sub-categories of Buddhism, some of which will be explored in following discussion.

The Introduction of Buddhism into China

Buddhism was introduced to China in the first century AD, during the Eastern Han dynasty, possibly through Buddhist merchants from India or central Asia. In the second century it had grown, such that there were Buddhist monks in several Chinese cities, and images of the Buddha became popular, promoting veneration of the Buddha. However the Eastern Han governments tried to control religion and especially disapproved of foreign religions. Therefore Buddhism only became more established and influential after the Han dynasty ended in the third century.[22]

According to Overmyer, Buddhism also took time to become accepted by the Chinese because it was very different to Chinese religions and mindset. Chinese traditions focussed on agriculture, family and community harmony, and prosperity in this life, rather than Buddhism's individualistic framework and focus on the next life. However Buddhism was also appealing to many Chinese people because it provided a simple system of morality, as well as philosophy for those who wished to learn it.[23]

Chinese forms of Buddhism

By the seventh century, two predominant Chinese forms of Buddhism had developed: Pure Land and Chan (known as Zen[24] in

---

[21] Dickson, p74-80.

[22] Overmyer, p43.

[23] Overmyer, p44.

[24] Ed. See Kate Lim's article on meditation in Zen Buddhism later in this present volume.

Japanese). Pure Land Buddhism works on the assumption that if people are reborn, then the Buddha must also have been reborn. Therefore there have been many Buddhas throughout the world's history. From this, the idea developed that there are many Buddhas in the world, one over each geographical area, or one that represents a particular Buddhist virtue. Amitabha was the name of the Buddha of compassion, and also supervises the Pure Land, or paradise. Pure Land Buddhists would not be required to meditate in the way that Gautama meditated, or even understand complex philosophy, but would pray to Amitabha and meditate on him. This would result in their salvation from purgatory or hell (teaching of which was present in some Buddhist scriptures), and they would go to the Pure Land, a wonderful place with no suffering, and where they could constantly listen to the Buddha's teaching, helping them attain enlightenment more easily. However the focus and appeal appeared to fall more on going to the Pure Land than Nirvana. The Pure Land movement was the most popular form of Buddhism in China in the 7th century, especially with peasants, as it gave assurance of salvation with less effort involved. Pure Land Buddhism also had significant support from many government officials and wealthy members of society, so it lost some focus on living simply and morally and of becoming aware and accepting of life circumstances. For these reasons, many of the more intellectual Chinese Buddhists began to dislike Pure Land Buddhism and developed Chan Buddhism in reaction to it.[25]

Chan Buddhists attempted to get back to teachings and practices of the Buddha, with a focus on meditation. Some Chan Buddhists went to small, remote monasteries to spend their time meditating. Chan was more accepted by Chinese intellectuals than peasants, perhaps because it required more effort to learn its philosophy, meditate and work towards Nirvana than Pure Land.

Ultimately, in Chan Buddhist thinking, the individual is responsible for achieving enlightenment themselves, and they have the means to achieve it. An implication of this is that a Chan Buddhist does not need to believe in anything in particular in order to achieve enlightenment. Their motto is: "Become a Buddha yourself by realizing your own inner potential."[26]

---

[25] Overmyer, pp44-46.
[26] Overmyer, p47.

The Integration of Buddhism and Chinese Religions

Once the Chinese accepted Buddhism more broadly, it appears to have integrated with Chinese culture and religions at many levels. As early as the fourth century, syncretism was encouraged by Chinese philosophers and scholars and by the tenth century Buddhism had become widely integrated into Chinese society.[27] There are several reasons for this integration.

First, Buddhism, Confucianism and Taoism are complementary and influence different aspects of life. Buddhism directs psychological development, due to meditation and the search for enlightenment; Taoist practice enhances the physical body; and Confucianism promotes good government and societal structure.[28] Since Confucianism, especially, is concerned with harmony in society, the Chinese were open to good new ideas that were also aimed at promoting harmony and unity. Buddhist teaching on abolishing desires should also lead to harmony, specifically, a lack of rebellion against government.

Secondly, the belief of many Buddhists is that there are many 'Buddhisms': "everyone 'must be a lamp unto themselves'; everyone must find their own way."[29] If this is a common belief, it seems natural that Buddhism would change and merge easily with other religions.[30] Buddhism is not bound to any particular culture and is also tolerant of other cultures and religions, because any good teaching ultimately came from the Buddha. In the *Books of Gradual Sayings*, the Buddha even encouraged his followers to make offerings to local gods, since it was important to local culture. As mentioned previously, Taoism and Confucianism are both concerned about the way to live harmoniously, rather than about specific spirituality or salvation, so it is feasible that a Buddhist can adhere to Buddhist beliefs but put them into practice through Confucianism, Taoism or traditional religions. Additionally, since

---

[27] X. Guang, "Buddhist Impact on Chinese Culture," *Asian Philosophy* 23, no. 4 (2013), p305 & 307.

[28] Guang, p307.

[29] J. Brodd, L. Little, B. Nystrom, R. Platzer, R. Shek, and E. Stiles, "Buddhism," *Invitation to World Religions,* vol. 1, Oxford University Press, 2013, p148.

[30] Guang, p306.

traditional or popular religions are not usually organised beliefs and practices, they tend to mix easily with more institutional religions. As a result, Buddhism shaped popular religions, but beliefs, gods and rituals from popular religions were also brought in to Buddhism, thereby creating 'Folk Buddhism'.[31]

Integration of Buddhism, Taoism and Confucianism was even deliberate in the sixteenth century, with the founding of the Three-in-One religion. Temples for this religion still exist in parts of South-east Asia.[32]

Buddhism and Taoism

Guang states that many Chinese scholars attribute the development of Taoism into a systematic religion, in part, to the introduction of Buddhism. As Buddhism was fairly developed when it reached China, with scriptures, practices and religious community, it motivated Taoist thinkers to organise and develop Taoism. In this process, some aspects of Buddhism were introduced into Taoism or else used as a model for Taoist thought and practice.[33] For example, Taoist thinkers merged the Buddha with the Shangqing creator god, calling it Yuanshi Tianzun (Heavenly Worthy of Primordial Beginning). This god also responds to philosophical questions, as does the Buddha.

Taoism had little clear teaching on life after death and Confucianism did not address it at all,[34] so Buddhism clarified the Chinese understanding of the after-life and reward or punishment for actions. The idea of being reborn as a god or ghost was already present amongst the Chinese, but the idea of being reborn as an animal as a result of one's actions was new. Some Taoist ideas of heaven and hell, including the names of the different levels of heaven and hell, are also taken from Buddhist names and sources.

---

[31] Leamaster and Hu, p236.

[32] E. Siegler, "Chinese Religions," in *Religions of the World: a comprehensive encyclopedia of beliefs and practices,* eds. J. Melton, et al.; Santa Barbara, California: ABC-CLIO, LLC, 2010, p260.

[33] Guang, p312-313.

[34] Siegler, p258.

Buddhism and Confucianism

While Buddhism may not have been incorporated into Confucianism, like with Taoism, it certainly complemented it or developed ideas in Chinese thinking generally that were not discussed in Confucianism. For example, Confucianism and early Chinese philosophy do not discuss death, whereas Buddhists are encouraged to talk about, meditate on and accept it as part of life.[35]

Buddhist teaching on karma gives a different explanation to Confucianism about reasons for good and bad fortune in life. Confucianism teaches that a person should fill the role in society that they are given (for example, husband or wife, teacher or student) and Taoism teaches that consequences of a person's actions are passed on to descendants, if not experienced by the person themselves. However Buddhism promotes the idea that a person will experience the consequences of their actions in their next life, and consequently in this life they are experiencing the effects of their actions in their past life.

This is a much more individualistic mindset than traditional Chinese thinking, particularly Confucianism, so it is interesting that the idea of individual karma became popular in China. It may well have been seen as an incentive to live morally and also gave comfort that people who were immoral would be punished, as Taoist teaching did not discuss punishment for bad deeds. However, as Guang points out, this kind of self-interest also promotes social harmony, since individuals are less likely to do bad things within their society if it will negatively affect them in their next life.[36]

Buddhism and Traditional (Popular) Religions

Even as early as 166AD, less than one century after Buddhism's introduction to China, there were altars to the Buddha and other Chinese philosophers, showing the merging of beliefs. Buddhist

---

[35] Guang, p311.
[36] Guang, p311.

bodhisattvas were introduced over time, and some were adapted to Chinese religions and deified. For example, Guanyin (or Kuan Yin) was originally a male Indian bodhisattva called Avalokiteśvara, but became known and worshipped in China as the goddess of mercy.[37] Maitreya (Chinese: Milefo), is also a very popular bodhisattva and has become known as the Chinese Laughing Buddha, representing "humanistic, practical and happy attitude of life with a spirit to promote peace and prosperity in society."[38]

A Buddhist influence on the idea of hell was also incorporated into popular belief. In Buddhism, there is a king over hell (Yama), which was expanded in Chinese thinking to ten kings over the different levels or parts of hell. People are taken to hell and punished for their wrong actions, presumably before being reborn. However, according to Buddhist teaching, one Bodhisattva has promised to deliver all people from hell. Therefore Chinese people may pray to him on behalf of their relatives.[39]

There is evidence of continuing folk Buddhism in China in the present day. Leamaster and Hu refer to a study conducted in 2003 in a village in Hebei Province, where Buddhism and popular religion were integrated to the extent that the villagers did not know which aspects came from Buddhism and which came from other beliefs.[40] Leamaster and Hu suggest that the level to which the two mix may be related to a person's connection to a Sangha (community or organisation of Buddhists, often linked to a Buddhist temple and the community of monks or nuns connected to it).[41] This is perhaps due to a person's level of commitment to Buddhism and education in its teachings. If a person is only loosely associated, or not associated at all, with a devout practising community of Buddhists, they may be less likely to be educated in Buddhist teachings.

Popular religion is practiced in modern times in a variety of ways. Annual festivals are a large part of Chinese life. Tomb-sweeping day

---

[37] Guang, p312-313. *A World Religions Reader*, I. S. Markham et al.(eds.), Malden, MA: Wiley-Blackwell, 2009, p96.

[38] Guang, p314.

[39] Guang, p313.

[40] Leamaster and Hu, p236.

[41] Leamaster and Hu, p236.

and Chinese New Year have roots in traditional religions, even if many secular Chinese do not realise it.[42] Common rituals include food sacrifices on household altars and divination; for example, the use of wooden blocks with one flat side and one curved side. The worshipper at a temple drops the two blocks on the ground and the side they land on indicates a yes or no answer.[43]

Leamaster and Hu conducted a survey across China regarding religious adherence and identified two groups of Buddhists: those who identify as Buddhists but have not formally committed to the religion, and those who have formally committed. They found that self-identifying Buddhists (termed as 'casual Buddhists') believe and practise popular religion, more than people identifying with another or no religion. However they also found that higher rates of formal Buddhists practise and believe popular religion, compared to casual Buddhists. This is possibly because formal Buddhists are generally more religious than casual Buddhists.[44] This indicates that both casual and formal Buddhists consider little or no problem with practising both kinds of religion. It also suggests that Buddhism and popular religion have become so mixed over the last two millennia that it is difficult to distinguish one from the other.[45]

Conclusion

China's religious history is very complex. Even before the introduction of Buddhism, there were some common beliefs shared by Taoism, Confucianism and traditional religions, though of course, differences as well. With the introduction of Buddhism, some of the Chinese beliefs and traditions were developed further, for example Taoism, and some were integrated with Buddhist teachings. In modern times, some aspects of Buddhism and traditional religions are indistinguishable to many Chinese people, resulting in the practice of folk Buddhism, or popular religion.

---

[42] Siegler, p260.

[43] Overmyer, p74.

[44] Leamaster and Hu, p252.

[45] Leamaster and Hu, p252.

DEMONIC TEMPTATION IN BUDDHISM AND ISLAM
with particular reference to Southeast Asia

Peter Riddell[1]

On face value, Buddhism and Islam do not have much in common. The former comes from the Indian cradle of faiths; the latter is Semitic. The former has a very nebulous God concept; the latter affirms a strict doctrine of the Oneness of the Creator God. The former is ambiguous about an afterlife; the latter paints the afterlife in graphic detail. The former shuns violence and war in its essential scripturalist form; the latter includes a doctrine of military jihad at the very core of its sacred texts.

However, such observations could lead us to ignore such parallels as do exist. The purpose of this paper is to focus on one such parallel, the concept that both faiths accommodate demonic temptation. Clearly this paper makes no suggestion of one faith influencing the other. Rather the discussion which follows is a study in comparative religions of a synchronic kind, rather than offering a diachronic search for common sources.

Lives of the founders

The Buddha was probably born in the 6th century before Christ, while Muhammad was born in the 6th century after Christ. It is difficult to separate fact from legend concerning the lives of both men. For Buddhists, who are more concerned with the message rather than the historical person of the Buddha, this does not pose a major problem. Not so with Muslims, who declare confidently that the somewhat idealized account of Muhammad's life presented

---

[1] Peter Riddell serves as Vice Principal Academic and Senior Research Fellow in Islam at MST. He has published extensively on Islam and Christian-Muslim Relations.

in the primary sources is historically accurate, in contrast with the available evidence that points to uncertainty.

The Buddha, born Siddhartha Gautama, entered the world as a prince of a small kingdom in southern Nepal. Muhammad was born into the dominant Quraysh tribe in Mecca in the Arabian Peninsula.

"Damascus Road" Experiences

According to tradition,[2] Siddhartha Gautama renounced his royal heritage at the age of 29 and sought to escape the cycle of birth, death, and rebirth that inevitably leads to suffering, loss, and pain. The traditional narrative relates that Siddhartha travelled widely in search of a spiritual guide. This quest proved fruitless, which led him to conclude that his faith context of Brahmanism did not provide the answer to his search for truth. Siddhartha then turned to extreme bodily asceticism, sitting for lengthy periods of time on a bed of thorns and eating little. He also found this a frustrating experience and concluded that asceticism was not the way to find truth. Then one night, at around the age of 35, Siddhartha sat under a fig tree, which became known as the *bo* or *bodhi* (enlightenment) tree.

> 'Siddhartha remained in meditation throughout the night, and during this time the veils of ignorance lifted from his perception... At dawn of the following morning, full awareness arose in him, and all traces of ignorance disappeared. He had become a 'buddha' ... he was now fully awakened from the sleep of ignorance in which most beings spend life after life."[3]

For Muhammad, the life-changing experience came around the age of 40 outside Mecca in a cave on Mount Hira. According to Islamic tradition, the angel Gabriel called on Muhammad to open his mouth and recite [or read] and, after some initial hesitation, Muhammad did so. The words that came from his mouth, considered by Muslims as God's direct speech, are recorded as the first five verses of chapter 96 of the Qur'an.

---

[2] For the traditional account of the Buddha's life, cf. David Burnett, *The Spirit of Buddhism*, London: Monarch, 2nd edn., 2003, pp15ff.

[3] John Powers and James Fieser, *Anthology of Scriptures of World Religions*, McGraw-Hill Publications, 1997, http://online.anu.edu.au/asianstudies/textnotes/buddhism.html, cited 30 August 2015.

*[The angel said] 'Read!' and I said 'What shall I read?' He pressed
me with it so tightly that I thought it was death; then he let me
go and said 'Read!' I said, 'What shall I read?' He pressed me
with it again so that I thought it was death, then he let me go and
said 'Read!' I said 'What shall I read?'— and this I said only to
deliver myself from him lest he should do the same to me again.
He said: 'Read in the name of thy Lord who created, who created
man of blood coagulated. Read! Thy Lord is the most beneficent,
who taught by the Pen, taught that which they knew not unto
men.'*[4]

From that time on, Muhammad renounced his secular activities as a
trader to take up a prophetic ministry.

The Founders Tempted
The Buddha tempted by Mara

Buddhist tradition relates that Mara, the evil spirit (or
personification of evil) in Buddhism, tempted Siddhartha while he
meditated beneath the *bodhi* tree. The attributes of Mara include
blindness, murkiness, death, and darkness. These attributes tried
to entice Siddhartha from the path of enlightenment by tempting
him to return to his former ways. Mara sent his three daughters —
Lust, Thirst, and Delight —to distract Siddhartha, to no avail. This
triggered a full scale assault on Siddharta.

"Mara attacked with a whirlwind, but that failed. He then caused
a rainstorm to drown Siddharta, but Siddharta didn't even get
wet. Next, he caused a shower of rocks, but the rocks changed
into bouquets, and a shower of weapons, but they became
celestial flowers. He cast a shower of live coals, but they came
down harmless, as did hot ashes, a shower of sand, and a shower
of mud. Finally, he caused a darkness, but the darkness
disappeared before the Buddha. With that, Mara fled, and
Siddharta became the Enlightened One."[5]

Muhammad tempted

[4] Alfred Guillaume (ed.), *The Life of Muhammad: A Translation of Ibn Ishaq's Sirat Rasul Allah*, Oxford: Oxford University Press, 2002, p106.

[5] http://www.deliriumsrealm.com/delirium/mythology/mara.asp, cited 6 July, 2005.

Just as the Buddha is tempted by demonic forces, Muhammad is subjected to various temptations, as recorded in Suras 113 and 114 of the Qur'an:[6]

> Sura 113:
> *1. Say [Prophet], 'I seek refuge with the Lord of daybreak*
> *2. against the harm in what He has created,*
> *3. the harm in the night when darkness gathers,*
> *4. the harm in witches when they blow on knots,*
> *5. the harm in the envier when he envies.'*
>
> Sura 114
> *1. Say, 'I seek refuge with the Lord of people,*
> *2. the Controller of people,*
> *3. the God of people,*
> *4. against the harm of the slinking whisperer --*
> *5. who whispers into the hearts of people--*
> *6. whether they be jinn or people.'*

Reference to Qur'an commentators helps to identify the sources of such temptations. Q113:4 above refers to witchcraft. In his translation and commentary on the Qur'an, which draws heavily on the classical Arabic commentaries by al-Baydawi (d. 1286) and the two Jalals (d. 1485 and 1505 respectively), George Sale explains that "the commentators relate that Lobeid, a Jew, with the assistance of his daughters, bewitched Mohammed, by tying eleven knots on a chord, which they hid in a well."[7] Furthermore, Q114:4 refers to "the slinking whisperer". Sale, drawing on his classical Arabic commentators, identifies this as Satan.[8]

So the temptations to which Muhammad was subjected involve both an adherent of a competitor faith (here a Jew) and Satan. This is a powerful device for setting up a natural connection in the minds of the Muslim faithful between Satan and other faiths, a theme which is developed later in this paper. If Muhammad was subjected to such temptation, how much more would ordinary Muslims be susceptible to the same, and need to find ways to ward off evil spirits.

---

[6] M. A. S. Abdel Haleem (trans.), *The Qur'an*, Oxford: Oxford University Press, 2005, pp445-6.

[7] George Sale, *The Koran*, London, 1734, p508.

[8] Sale, p508.

Ongoing temptation for the faithful
The Continuing Temptations of Mara

According to Buddhist tradition, a process of textual codification was carried out by a council assembled of 500 of Buddha's followers shortly after his death.[9] There were no written records of his teachings, so oral records were drawn upon. One of the results was the *Dhammapada*, a text that has a key role in today's Buddhist practice. It consists of 423 verses in Pali purportedly uttered by the Buddha on some 305 occasions to diverse audiences, selected and compiled into one book. It is divided into 26 chapters and the stanzas are arranged according to subject matter. It serves as an effective vehicle for providing a model for future generations of Buddhists.

In Buddhist belief, Mara wanders the earth capturing the souls of the dying. He is an ongoing tempter, trying to lure monks, nuns and other seekers away from the path of enlightenment even today.[10]

> "Mara is the ruler of desire and death, the two evils that chain man to the wheel of ceaseless rebirth. Mara reviles man, blinds him, guides him toward sensuous desires; once man is in his bondage, Mara is free to destroy him."[11]

The *Dhammapada* wastes no time in introducing Mara, so central is the tempter. First mention is made at the very outset, in Canto I:

7. "The pleasure-seeker who finds delight in physical objects, whose senses are unsubdued, who is immoderate in eating, indolent and listless, him Mara (the Evil One) prevails against, as does the monsoon wind against a weak-rooted tree.

8. He who perceives no pleasure in physical objects, who has perfect control of his senses, is moderate in eating, who is

---

[9] Most Buddhist scholars dispute the historicity of this event. Cf. Charles S. Prebish, "Councils, Buddhist", in Robert E. Buswell, Jr. et. al. (eds.), *Encyclopedia of Buddhism*, New York: Macmillan Reference USA, 2004, pp187-8.

[10] Burnett, p95.

[11] http://www.angelfire.com/electronic/bodhidharma/mara.html, cited 6 July 2005.

unflinching in faith, energetic, him Mara does not prevail against any more than does the wind against a rocky mountain."[12]

The *Dhammapada* allocates all of Canto IX to the issue of evil, thereby providing an ongoing and significant role for the tempter in the lives of the faithful. The text reads as follows:

Evil – CANTO IX[13]

116. Make haste in doing good and restrain the mind from evil; if one is slow in doing good, the mind finds delight in evil.

117. If a man commits evil let him not repeat it again and again; let him not delight in it, for the accumulation of sin brings suffering.

118. If a man commits a meritorious deed, let him perform it again and again; let him develop a longing for doing good; happiness is the outcome of the accumulation of merit.

119. Even the wrongdoer finds some happiness so long as (the fruit of) his misdeed does not mature; but when it does mature, then he sees its evil results.

120. Even the doer of good deeds knows evil (days) so long as his merit has not matured; but when his merit has fully matured, then he sees the happy results of his meritorious deeds.

121. Do not think lightly of evil, saying, "It will not come to me." By the constant fall of waterdrops, a pitcher is filled; likewise the unwise person, accumulating evil little by little, becomes full of evil.

122. Do not think lightly of merit, saying, "It will not come to me." By the constant fall of waterdrops, a pitcher is filled; likewise the wise person, accumulating merit little by little, becomes full of merit.

123. As a merchant who has limited escort, yet carries much wealth, avoids a perilous road, as a man who is desirous of living long avoids poison, so in the same way should the wise shun evil.

124. If one does not have a wound in his hand, he may carry poison in his palm. Poison does not affect him who has no wound. There is no ill effect for the person who does no wrong.

125. Whoever offends an innocent, pure and faultless person, the evil (of his act) rebounds on that fool, even as fine dust thrown against the wind.

---

[12] "The Twin Verses -- CANTO I", *Dhammapada, Wisdom of the Buddha*, trans. Harischandra Kaviratna, Theosophical University Press Online Edition, http://www.theosociety.org/pasadena/dhamma/dham1.htm#Canto1, cited 6 July 2005.

[13] "Evil -- CANTO IX", *Dhammapada, Wisdom of the Buddha*, http://www.theosociety.org/pasadena/dhamma/dham9.htm#Canto9, cited 6 July 2005.

126. (After death), some are reborn in the womb; evildoers are born in hell; those who commit meritorious deeds go to heaven; and those who are free from worldly desires realize nirvana.

127. Not in the sky, not in the middle of the ocean, not even in the cave of a mountain, should one seek refuge, for there exists no place in the world where one can escape the effects of wrongdoing.

128. Not in the sky, not in the middle of the ocean, not even in the cave of a mountain, should one seek refuge, for there exists no place in the world where one will not be overpowered by death.

Mara represents the antithesis of the Buddha, representing carnal desires in contrast with Buddha's call to shun worldly preoccupations.

We will devote the remainder of this paper to the Southeast Asian context, where both Buddhism and Islam flourished at different points in time. We will see that the themes of temptation discussed in general terms in preceding paragraphs were given a particular focus in the Southeast Asian region.

Temptation in Stone: the Borobudur in Indonesia

Buddhism filtered into the Indonesian archipelago, first arriving perhaps in the 4th – 5th centuries AD. Chinese traveller reports suggest that the 6th and 7th centuries were crucial in the consolidation of Buddhism in Indonesia.[14] One of the most significant Buddhist kingdoms was that of Mataram in Central Java, ruled by the Sailendra dynasty in the 8th and 9th centuries.

The Sailendras were major temple builders, with arguably their most spectacular achievement being the temple of Borobudur, considered as one of the Seven Wonders of the World.[15] The 7th and 8th centuries heralded significant temple construction throughout Buddhist India, Ceylon and South East Asia. Following on this tradition, the Sailendras built the Borobudur temple over a period of 80 years in the 9th century.

---

[14] Natasha Reichle, *Violence and Serenity: Late Buddhist Sculpture from Indonesia*, Honolulu: University of Hawaii Press, 2007, pp15ff.

[15] http://www.buddhanet.net/e-learning/buddhistworld/indo-txt.htm, cited 5 July 2005.

The Borobudur is an enormous structure, with a base measuring 120 metres square and a height of 35 metres. The temple was built to resemble a microcosm of the universe. It provided visual representation of the Buddha's teachings, presenting the steps that each individual needed to follow in order to achieve enlightenment.

The temple was abandoned after a severe earthquake and a large volcanic eruption of Mount Merapi in 1006 AD, but after a lengthy period of decay, it was rediscovered by Thomas Stamford Raffles during the British inter-regnum in Indonesia in 1814.

Siddharta subjected to attack from Mara and the legions of demons[16]

Some 1,460 narrative bas-relief carvings appear in the galleries of the five concentric square terraces of the Temple representing different stages in the Buddha's journey to enlightenment. The two illustrations here are representative.

---

[16] Die Buddha-Legende auf den flachreliefs der ersten galerie des stupa von Boro-budur Java, Leipzig: Otto Harrassowitz, 1923.
http://luk.staff.ugm.ac.id/Borobudur/relief/Wilsen/19.html#094, cited 8 September 2015.

Mara's daughters tempt Siddharta[17]

As pilgrims progress through the different levels of the Borobudur, the carved representation of Buddha's path to enlightenment provides a model for the goal of individual Buddhists in shunning evil and seeking to follow the path. Individuals are therefore reminded of the role of Mara the tempter in their own lives when encountering scenes at the temple such as in the above diagrams.

'Abd al-Ra'uf's *Lubb al-kashf*

Remaining in Southeast Asia but turning our attention to Islam, the theme of temptation occurs in a striking fashion in the writing of 'Abd al-Ra'uf of Singkel (ca. 1615 - ca. 1693). He is arguably the most important Islamic scholar from the Malay world to have lived during the formative stages of Malay Islam. He left a detailed record of his nineteen year study visit (1642-1661) to the various centres of Islamic learning in the Arabian penninsula. His prolific literary output, in wide-ranging fields of Islamic learning, provided succeeding generations of Malay students of Islam with copious materials for study.

One of his shorter works which bears directly on the subject of this paper is *Lubb al-kashf wa al-bayan lima yarahu al-muhtadar bi al-'iyan*[18] (Essential exposition and Clarification on the Visionary Experience of the Dying and what Gladdens him) which describes

---

[17] Die Buddha-Legende auf den flachreliefs der ersten galerie des stupa von Boro-budur Java, http://luk.staff.ugm.ac.id/Borobudur/relief/Wilsen/19.html#095, cited 8 September, 2015.

[18] P. Voorhoeve, "Bajan Tadjalli", *Tijdschrift voor Indische Taal-, Land- en Volkenkunde*, 23, 1952, pp91-99.

the experience of the dying.[19] 'Abd al-Ra'uf begins his text in the first person. It reads as follows:

> In the name of Allah I begin reading this document ... I found it within a Jawi text, addressing what happens to a person when he dies. It is as follows:

> When a person is at the point of death[20] he experiences several visions.[21] When a vision of black appears to him, which is Satan, then he should utter [the creed] "There is no God but Allah and Muhammad is the prophet of Allah, He, He, He."[22] When a vision of red appears to him, which represents the Christians, then he should utter "There is no God but Allah and Muhammad is the prophet of Allah, He, He, He." When a vision of yellow appears to him, which represents the Jews, then he should utter "There is no God but Allah and Muhammad is the prophet of Allah, He, He, He". When a vision of white appears to him, which represents the vision of our prophet Muhammad the messenger of Allah, then he should utter "By the will of Allah he was one of the true believers".

> After that, there comes [a vision] between the eyebrows of the person who is on the point of death, like the full moon in the evening [after a cycle] of fourteen days,[23] its brightness filling the Seven Heavens and Earth, containing a vision of ourselves. It proceeds with an exposition, the like of which I have never witnessed in all the books of Hadith and the writings of the Sufis. ... I have only found such an exposition on the experience of death in the work Tadhkira by Shaykh Jamal al-Din ... ibn Muhammad ibn Ahmad Qurtubi. Shaykh Jamal al-Din ... relates in the work Tadhkira the following account from the scholars.

> When a servant of Allah is at the point of death, two devils sit next to him, one on his right and one on his left. The devil on his right takes the form of his father, and says to him: "O my child, I truly love and cherish you. Please die in the Christian faith, as it is the best of religions." The devil on his left takes the form of his

---

[19] Ed. Compare this with Ian Schoonwater's discussion earlier in this volume.

[20] Ar. *sakara al-mawt*, ref. Q50:19.

[21] These represent temptations, designed to direct the Muslim away from Islam.

[22] The 3rd person singular pronoun is a further reference to Allah. Thus the Muslim avoids the tempter by pronouncing the Creed, which affirms his faith.

[23] The full moon takes approximately fifteen days to appear after the sighting of the new moon.

mother, and says to him: "O my child, my womb was your shelter, my milk was your nourishment and my lap was your place of repose. Please die in the Jewish faith, as it is the best of religions."

Moreover, it states that Iblis[24] orders his soldiers to visit the person at the point of death and to confuse him. So they come to the person at the point of death, and they present themselves to the person in the form of all his loved ones who died before him, of those who guided him during his life, such as his father, mother, brothers, sisters, and friends who cared for him. They say to him: "O so-and-so. You are dying. We have already undergone the experience of death before you. So please die in the Jewish faith, for it is the faith which is pleasing to Allah." If the person turns away and does not wish to comply with the urgings of the devils, another group of devils comes to him and says: "O so-and-so, please die in the Christian faith, for it is the religion of the Messiah, namely Jesus, which through him abrogated the religion of Moses." These [devils] proceed to list for him all the beliefs of each religion.

Thereupon Allah inclines whoever He wishes towards faiths which have gone astray. This is in accordance with Allah's decree: *rabbana la tuzigh qulubana ba'da idh hadaytana,*[25] i.e. "Our Lord! Do not incline our hearts to faiths which have gone astray at our moment of death after You have shown us the true faith beforehand, namely during our lives." Whenever Allah wishes to show one of His servants the true path and to affirm him through statement of the Divine Unity, the angel of mercy comes to him - some scholars identify him as Gabriel - and he drives away from that person all the devils, and he wipes his face, and the person smiles from time to time. We can observe that the majority of people at the point of death smile in the grave while rejoicing at receiving the good account from Allah's angel of mercy. The angel of mercy says to him: "O so-and-so, you do not know me. I am Gabriel, and they are your enemy, Satan. Please die in the faith which is pure and the law which is true." Nothing is more cherished or more hoped for by a person than that the angel of mercy comes to him. This is in accordance with Allah's decree: *wahab lana min ladunka rahmatan innaka*

---

[24] Ed. "Iblis" is the transliteration of an Arabic synonym for Satan, also called "Shaytan" in Arabic; considered a 'jinn' or (evil) spirit.

[25] Q3:8.

anta al-wahhab,[26] i.e. "My Lord, grant us mercy from Your presence. You alone are the Lord who is most bountiful."

Thereupon the angel of death draws out the soul of that person.

Reflections on the text

Lubb al-kashf wa al-bayan provides an interesting insight into how the prophetic model affects the life of the ordinary faithful. Chapters 113 and 114 of the Qur'an describe how Muhammad was subjected to temptations and witchcraft. Similarly, ordinary believers are subjected to temptations throughout life, with the focus of this text referring specifically to the end of life experience. The tempters are demonic forces seeking to lead the believer away from Islam.

However, an additional element is introduced in this Islamic context, compared with the ongoing temptations for the Buddhist believer described above. In *Lubb al-kashf* a clear link is drawn between demonic temptation and non-Islamic faiths, with tempters seeking to draw the believer not only away from Islam but into the religions of Judaism or Christianity. This co-location of demonic temptation with other faiths has significant ramifications for the view of some Muslims towards other faiths.

Conclusions

As stated at the outset, no suggestion is being made by this paper that resemblances between Buddhism and Islam point to common ancestry. However, it is certainly interesting to note generic parallels between two unrelated faiths as we are seeing here. Both the Buddha and Muhammad represented reformers, seeking to identify a better path than that offered by the faiths existing around them. Both the Buddha and Muhammad claimed special spiritual experiences through withdrawal to an isolated location. Both men claimed to have undergone a period of temptation – and emergence from that temptation – during their lives.[27] Furthermore, the temptations experienced by both men were not unique to them; on

---

[26] Q3:8.

[27] Parallels with Jesus are also striking here.

the contrary, the sources of such temptation are enduring, and continue to work in the lives of the faithful who follow them. A unique dimension to Islam is that the forces for temptation to do evil are specifically and overtly associated with other faiths: Judaism and Christianity in this case.

Such are the helpful observations that can emerge from a study of comparative religion. These observations raise questions about the generic nature of certain claims by charismatic religious reformers, regardless of their context. This question requires further thought and further research.

ISLAM and JUDAISM:
the depiction of the Jews
from the Qur'an and the Hadith

Bernie Power[1]

Introduction

Relationships between Muslims and Jews and their attitudes towards each other are key to understanding the Middle East. Both religions are based on a revelation and accompanying traditions and commentary which have established the foundation for how they view each other. This paper will examine how Muslims might view Jews based on the earliest Islamic documents.

The Qur'an is the sourcebook for Islam: it is the only reliable revelation from Allah, according to Muslims. Second only to the Qur'an is the Hadith: that assorted collection of traditions which helps us understand the thinking of the Prophet Muhammad and his earliest followers on a variety of topics. What the Qur'an and the Hadith teach about Jews and Judaism has abiding relevance, and influences Muslim assessments of the Jews, even up until today. It is the goal of this paper to explore the range of views about Jews found in the Qur'an and the Hadith.

The Qur'an's depiction of the Jews

There are over 600 Qur'anic verses which give information about the Jews.[2] Considering that the Qur'an has about 6200 verses, this is a substantial emphasis.

---

[1] Bernie Power worked with Interserve for 21 years in Asia and the Middle East. He lectures in Islamic Studies at the Melbourne School of Theology, and works with CultureConnect in Melbourne. His doctorate was on the Hadith, resulting in three books. His next book is about the Qur'an.

[2] There are 637 verses which relate to the Jewish people (sometimes including 'the People of the Book') or Jewish history (including Moses and the Jewish kings) or the Torah (including 'that which was before [the Qur'an]') They are - **1**:7; **2**:40-147, 211; **3**:3,4,19-25, 50, 64-102,

Titles of the Jews

The Jews are called by a range of names. The most common title is 'the children of Israel' (*bani/isrā'īl*),[3] and often they are bracketed with the Christians (and Sabeans) as *ahl al-kitāb*, 'the people of the book'.[4] They are also called 'the Jews' (*al-yahūd*)[5] or 'those who were guided' (*alladhīn hādū*)[6] or 'Jews' (*hūd*ᵃⁿ)[7].

The Qur'an speaks of the Jews as two communities: those which existed previously, especially during the time of Moses and Jesus, and those who lived when the Qur'an was being revealed by Muhammad. Sometimes the two communities are conflated by implying that the later Jews were simply following the earlier Jews in their disobedience towards Allah. At other times a distinction is made between them to imply that the promises made to the earlier Jews no longer applied to the later Jews as a result of continued disobedience. There are many descriptions of exchanges between Muhammad and the Jews of his time.

Part 1: Positive views about the Jews

Some verses present the Jews in a positive light.

Their privileged status

The advantages of the Jews are outlined. According to the Qur'an, Allah 'favoured' (literally 'graced' *an'amt* – the same verb as applied to the believers in 1:7) the Jews[8] and 'preferred them over the worlds (*al-ālamīn*).'[9] The commentator Ibn Kathir notes that

---

110-120, 181-188; **4:**45-56, 60, 153-169; **5:**12-26, 32, 41-82; **6:**91,92,146,154; **7:**128,137-156, 159-171; **9:**29-34; **10:**37; **12:**111; **16:**43,118; **17:**2-8, 101-104; **20:**9-97; **21:**48, 78-81, 105; **22:**17; **23:**45-49; **25:**35,36; **26:**10-68; **27:**7-44; **28:**3-55, 76-82; **29:**27, 9, 40, 46, 47; **32:**23-25; **33:**26,27; **34:**10-14; **37:**114-132; **38:**17-40; **40:**22-33; **41:**45; **43:**46-56; **45:**16,17; **46:**12; **48:**29; **51:**38-40; **57:**16, 28,29; **59:**2-17; **61:**5,14; **98:**1-6.

[3] 40 times e.g. 2:40; 61:14.

[4] This phrase occurs 33 times in the Qur'an.

[5] 2:113,120; 5:18,51,64,82; 9:30.

[6] 2:62; 4:46,160; 5:41,44, 69; 6:146; 7:156; 16:118; 22:17; 62:6.

[7] 2:111,135,140.

[8] 2:40.

[9] 2:40,47,122; 45:16.

al- ālamīn "encompasses everything in existence except Allah. ... all that has a mind, the Jinns, mankind, the angels and the devils, but not the animals...all that Allah has created with a soul."[10]

This positive preference towards the Jews by Allah manifested itself in action. Through the leadership of Moses and by mighty miracles,[11] Allah saved them from the tyrannical rule of Pharoah, caused them to inherit the treasure of Egypt,[12] and then brought them through the Red Sea.[13] They escaped into the desert, where Allah provided water from springs[14] and manna and quails and protected them with clouds.[15]

He established a mutual covenant with them.[16] He gave them the scripture,[17] and many clear verses/signs,[18] as well as the laws, prophethood and provision.[19] He also entrusted them with the protection of His book.[20]

Even after they sinned by asking Moses 'to show them Allah clearly', and were all killed by lightning,[21] Allah raised them from the dead.[22] He granted them the Promised Land.[23] Allah gave power to those who believed, and they were victorious.[24] In the following years, Allah sent them messengers.[25] He appointed twelve leaders over them and told them to perform the prayers, give alms, believe in the messengers by honouring and assisting them, and to give a

---

[10] http://www.qtafsir.com/index.php?option=com_content&task=view&id=78&Itemid=35
[11] 7:130-137.
[12] 26:58,59.
[13] 2:49,50; 17:101-103; 20:77-80.
[14] 2:60; 7:160.
[15] 2:57,60; 7:160; 20:80,81.
[16] 2:40, 83; 4:154; 5:12, 70; 20:80.
[17] 40:53; 32:23.
[18] 2:211.
[19] 29:27; 45:16.
[20] 5:44.
[21] 2:55.
[22] 2:56.
[23] 5:21; 2:58; 7:161; 17:104; possibly 26:57-59.
[24] 61:14.
[25] 5:70.

goodly loan to Allah.[26] He gave them wise and mighty kings like David and Solomon. Allah promised to forgive their sins if they repented,[27] and He forgave them after they sinned.[28] If it had not been for the grace and mercy of Allah, they would have been 'losers' (*khāsirīn*).[29]

Along with Christians and Sabaeans, the Jews are accorded a privileged status as 'people of the book'. However it is suggested that some of these privileges might belong only to the Jews of the distant past. "That was a nation that passed away. They will receive the reward of what they earned, and you [the current generation of Jews in Medina] of what you earn."[30] Moreover it is also questioned whether Abraham, Ishmael, Isaac, Jacob and 'the [twelve] tribes' (*al-asbāṭ*) were Jews (or Christians). Muhammad tells the Jews of his day that Allah knows better the truth about this matter.[31]

Obligations of the Jews

The privileged status accorded to the Jews brought along with it some responsibilities. They were required to fulfil their covenant, and to fear only Allah.[32] They had to worship Allah alone, show kindness to their parents, relatives, orphans and the poor, speak well to the people, perform prayers and give alms.[33] They must not act corruptly and make mischief on the earth.[34] Although the law of retaliation 'life for life, eye for eye, nose for nose, ear for ear, tooth for tooth, and equal wounds' was ordained for them, they could remit this privilege by way of charity, so it would become an expiation for their sins.[35]

However for those living in Muhammad's time, a new set of obligations now arose because of the new revelation. They had to

---

[26] 5:12.

[27] 2:58.

[28] 2:52.

[29] 2:64.

[30] 2:134, 141.

[31] 2:140.

[32] 2:40, 41.

[33] 2:83.

[34] 2:60.

[35] 5:45.

believe what had been sent down (i.e. the Qur'anic verses) because it confirmed what was with them (i.e. the Torah),[36] and to judge by what Allah has revealed.[37] They were told, as people of the book, that: "You have nothing until you stand on (or act according to) the Torah, Injil and what has been sent down to you from your Lord."[38] They were also told not to sell Allah's verses for a small price.[39]

Teaching about the Torah

The Qur'an gives several descriptions of the Torah outlined in the table on the next page. All of these, except one ('guide' *imām*) are identical with ways that the Qur'an describes itself.

The Torah (i.e. Pentateuch), *mazmur* (i.e. Psalms), and *injil* (i.e. Gospels) were books revealed by Allah.[40] The Torah was given to the Jews "so that you might be rightly guided."[41] It was "a reminder for those who keep from evil."[42] "Whoso judges not by that which Allah has revealed: such are disbelievers."[43] The Qur'an states that each successive scripture confirms its predecessor,[44] with the Gospel confirming the Torah.[45] The ultimate book, the Qur'an, confirms all the holy books which came before it.[46]

Were they 'saved' as Jews?

Some verses imply that Jews were on the path of salvation by following their religion. Since the Torah contained guidance and light, (as well as all the other characteristics mentioned above), the Jews of Muhammad's time were called to judge themselves by the Torah.[47] Jews, along with Christians and Muslims, have been given

---

[36] 2:41.

[37] 5:45.

[38] 5:68.

[39] 2:41.

[40] 4:163-65, 5:46-48; 6:91-92.

[41] 2:53.

[42] 21:48.

[43] 5:44.

[44] 2:42; 3:3; 12:111; 46:12.

[45] 5:46.

[46] 2:41,89, 91,97,101; 3:3,50,81; 4:47; 5:46,48; 6:92; 10:37; 12:111; 35:31; 46:12,30; 61:6.

[47] 5:44.

a law and a clear way to follow. Allah could have made them all one nation, but He wanted to test each of them, so they must compete in good deeds.[48] By following the revelation that they had, as long they

DESCRIPTION		Applied to the Torah
Book *kitāb*	كِتَاب	2:87; 6:91,154; 17:2; 25:35; 28:43; 33:23; 37:117 40:53; 41:45; 45:16
Remembrance *dhikr*	ذِكْر	2:63; 21:48, 105; 37:168; 40:54 *ahl al-dhikr* = 16:43; 21:7,48
Guidance *hudā*	هُدَى	5:44; 6:91,154; 7:154; 28:43; 32:23;40:53,54
Mercy *raḥma*	رَحْمَة	6:154; 7:154; 28:43
Criterion *furqān*	فُرْقان	2:53; 21:48
Light nūr	نُور	5:44; 6:91
Word (of God) *kalām*	كلام	2:75; 7:144
Guide *imām*	إِمَاماً	46:12
Lamp *diyā'*	ضِياء	21:48
Wisdom *ḥikma*	حِكْمَة	4:54
Clear signs *ayyāt bayyināt*	أَيَّات بيّنات	17:101
Command *amr*	أمر	7:150
Enlightenment *baṣā'ir*	بَصَائر	28:43

---

[48] 5:48.

believed and did good works, Jews, Christians, Sabeans, and Muslims would not fear nor grieve on the Last Day.[49] However, this appears to be in conflict with other verses which tell the Jews to "fear the Day" when no person, intercession, compensation or help will avail them.[50] The Qur'an also states that "the religion with Allah is Islam",[51] and "Whoever seeks a religion other than Islam, it will never be accepted of him, and in the hereafter he will be one of the losers,"[52] and that Islam will prevail over all other religions.[53]

Some of the Jews of Muhammad's time accepted Islam

Despite their privileges and the testimony of the Torah, all Jews were not obedient to Allah's call: the Qur'an states that "many of them became blind and deaf."[54] The vast majority of the Jews who came into contact with Muhammad did not embrace Islam, "most of them do not believe",[55] despite his preaching to them. It was said of them: "Some are on the right path, but many do evil deeds,"[56] or "a group of the Children of Israel believed, and a group disbelieved.[57]

But some Jews did believe in the teaching of the Qur'an.[58] They were described as those who "are well-grounded in knowledge. They believe in what has been sent down to Muhammad and what was sent down before, perform prayers, give *zakāt* and believe in Allah and the Last Day.[59] One of them was "a learned scholar of the children of Israel."[60] He is commonly identified as Abdullah bin Salām, who embraced Islam in Medina. Those Jews and Christians who accepted the Qur'an stated that they had been following Islam

---

[49] 2:62; 5:69.
[50] 2:48.
[51] 3:19.
[52] 3:85.
[53] 9:33; 48:28,29; 61:9.
[54] 5:71.
[55] 2:100.
[56] 5:66.
[57] 61:14; 4:55.
[58] 29:47.
[59] 4:162.
[60] 26:197.

beforehand. They said: "We believe in it. It is the truth from our Lord. And we were Muslims before it."[61]

Part 2: Negative views about the Jews

The majority of the verses in the Qur'an which describe the Jews present them in a bad light. They are called "the strongest among men in enmity towards the believers", and classified along with the polytheists (*mushrikīn*).[62] What did they do to deserve this categorization?

Jews are criticised for and accused of a range of behaviours

(a) Historical: the earlier communities of Jews
Although saved out of Egypt and taken by Moses into the safety of the desert, the Jews quickly became disobedient. They said to Moses: "We will not believe in you until we see Allah plainly."[63] They worshipped a golden calf,[64] and they were wrong-doers (*ẓālimīn*).[65] Moses ordered them to kill each other as a repentance.[66] They argued and disputed with Moses about what type of cow to offer for sacrifice, eventually complying. When they killed a man, resulting in a dispute, they were ordered to strike him with a piece of the cow, and he came back to life. Despite this their hearts became hardened like stone.[67] They complained about the food in the desert.[68] Allah commanded them not to transgress the Sabbath,[69] but they disobeyed the Sabbath law.[70] For breaking the covenant, Allah raised the Mount (Sinai?) over them (as a threat).[71]

---

[61] 28:53.
[62] 5:82.
[63] 2:55; 4:153.
[64] 2:51,54,92; 4:153; 7:148, 152; 20:86-88.
[65] 2:51.
[66] 2:54.
[67] 2:67-74.
[68] 2:61.
[69] 4:154.
[70] 2:65; 4:154,155; 7:163.
[71] 2:58; 4:154.

When the report of the strength of the inhabitants of the 'holy land' (*al-arḍ al-muqaddasa*) came back, the Jews refused to enter it, so they had to wander in the desert for forty years.[72] He said: "Enter the gate (of Jerusalem?) prostrating with humility, asking for Allah's forgiveness.[73] When they entered the town prostrating, they mockingly changed the word Allah had given them to say to another one.[74] They slid back, "except a few of them."[75] One passage seems to allude to invasions of Israel's land by foreign powers and the destruction of the Temple (here it is called 'the mosque' (*al-masjid*).[76] Certainly the Jews did not follow the example of Abraham who submitted to Allah. He was connected with Mecca, even rebuilding the house of Allah, the *Ka'ba*. His sons worshipped Allah only, but that nation or community (*umma*) passed away, to be replaced by the current Jews.[77]

Their lack of faith continued throughout Jewish history: they are called disbelievers (*kāfirīn*)[78] or those who believe only a little (*qalīlan mā yu'minūn*).[79] They thought there would be no coming trial or punishment (*fitna*) so they became blind and deaf. Even though Allah turned to them, many of them again became blind and deaf.[80] They said they would not believe a prophet unless he brought an offering which would be devoured with fire (from heaven).[81] They were ordered to fight, but turned away.[82]

They called the prophets liars,[83] and killed many of the messengers that Allah sent to them.[84] When the Messiah was born, they disbelieved and uttered a false charge against Mary, the mother of

---

[72] 5:21-26.

[73] 2:58; 4:154.

[74] 2:58,59. The Hadith state that the new word was a mockery of what Allah had said.

[75] 2:83.

[76] 17:4-7.

[77] 2:124-134.

[78] 2:61, 89, 93; 2:211.

[79] 2:88.

[80] 5:71.

[81] 3:183.

[82] 2:246.

[83] 5:70.

[84] 2:61, 87, 91; 3:21, 112, 181, 183; 4:155; 5:70.

Jesus.[85] At the end of the Messiah's life, they claimed that they had killed him, but they were mistaken. They have no knowledge and they follow nothing but conjecture.[86]

(b) the current Jewish community, during the revelation of the Qur'an:

When Muhammad migrated to Medina, he came into contact with the three Jewish tribes residing there. The strongest criticism of the Jews was a result of this contact. There are many denunciations of the Jews for a variety of reasons given below.

(i) How the Jews responded to and treated the Torah

The first charge was that of duplicity regarding the Torah, as illustrated through a range of behaviours: it was said that they conceal the truth and mix falsehood with truth,[87] and that they concealed and effaced the teaching of their book.[88] For example, they write the book with their own hands and claim: "This is from Allah",[89] or they distort the Book with their tongues, to give them impression that their words are from Allah.[90] They believe in a part of the Scripture and reject the rest.[91] Some of them threw away the book of Allah behind their backs, as if they did not know it.[92] But Allah knows what they reveal and what they conceal.[93] It was stated that they change the words of Allah[94] from their places,[95] and they sell the verses of Allah "for a small price".[96] On the other hand, some are unlettered and do not know the book at all.[97]

---

[85] 4:156.
[86] 4:157.
[87] 2:42,140,146; 3:71.
[88] 5:15.
[89] 2:79.
[90] 3:78.
[91] 2:85.
[92] 2:101.
[93] 2:77.
[94] 2:59,75; 3:78; 5:13, 41; 7:162.
[95] 5:41.
[96] 2:41,79; 5:44.
[97] 2:78.

(ii) Allegations of greed and the desire for money

It is stated that the Jews are the greediest in life, even greedier than the idolators.[98] They chose the goods of this low life,[99] because they love this world and do not care about eternity.[100] Their activities include the taking of usury (*ribā*),[101] and devouring men's wealth unlawfully.[102] As a result, they have sold themselves.[103] They bought the life of this world at the price of the Hereafter,[104] so they all wanted to live one thousand years.[105] They even claimed arrogantly: "Allah is poor and we are rich."[106]

(iii) Fighting

The Jews were accused of belligerence and violence. Even though they had a covenant with Allah not to shed the blood of their own people or turn them out of their houses, they killed one another, drove them out of their houses, assisted their enemies and ransomed their captives.[107] With other communities, they start wars and cause trouble on the earth.[108] Yet they do not engage in honourable combat: they are cowards, fighting only behind walls in fortified villages.[109]

There are descriptions of the defeat by the Muslims of the three Jewish tribes in Medina: the Bani Qaynuqa,[110] the Bani Nadir[111] (who were exiled from Medina after their date crop was burned by Muslims during the siege of their fortress), and the Bani Qurayza[112]

---

98 2:96.

99 7:169.

100 2:96.

101 4:161.

102 4:161.

103 2:90.

104 2:86.

105 2:96.

106 3:181.

107 2:85.

108 5:64.

109 59:14.

110 59:15.

111 59:2-6.

112 33:26,27.

(whose men were executed by beheading and women and children enslaved).

(iv) Personal behaviour

According to the Qur'an, most Jews could not be trusted. They break compacts, forget their revelation, and engage in treachery, except for a few of them.[113] They even broke their covenant with Allah.[114] Although Allah told them to 'Hold fast', they turned away.[115] They reject the signs of Allah,[116] and tell a lie against Him.[117] They listen much and eagerly to lies, falsehood and anything forbidden.[118] Some people of the Book want to lead Muslims astray,[119] and they hindered many from Allah's way.[120] They do not love Muslims unless the Muslim converts to their religion.[121] They are described as the enemies of the Muslims.[122]

Yet their own faith is weak. They are hypocrites[123] and not believers.[124] Most of them do not believe.[125] They claimed 'We believe' but they entered and exited Muslims' houses with the same disbelief.[126] Their behaviour reflected this. They hurried towards sin and transgression and they ate illegal food,[127] even though their rabbis and scholars should have prevented them from doing these things.[128] They had made up their own rules. According to the Qur'an, "all food was made lawful to the children of Israel, except

---

[113] 5:13; 4:100.
[114] 2:84,85,100; 4:155; 5:13.
[115] 2:63,64.
[116] 4:155.
[117] 3:75.
[118] 5:41,42.
[119] 2:109; 3:69-72.
[120] 4:160.
[121] 2:120.
[122] 4:45,46.
[123] 2:14, 44, 76.
[124] 5:43.
[125] 2:100.
[126] 5:61.
[127] 5:62.
[128] 5:63.

what Israel made unlawful for himself before the Torah was revealed."[129]

They were impertinent towards Muhammad, insulting him.[130] They came to Muhammad for decisions even though they already had the Torah as a guide, and then they simply turned away.[131] They challenged Muhammad to make a book descend upon them from heaven.[132] They played mocking word games: they said "We hear and obey" (rā'inā) in Arabic, knowing that it was an insult in Hebrew.[133] The revelation from Allah simply increased in most of them their obstinate rebellion and disbelief.[134]

(v) They made outrageous statements

The Qur'an states that the Jews claimed Ezra is the son of God.[135] They accused Allah of having tied hands, and so lacking in bounty.[136] It was commonly believed that everyone would spend some time in hell suffering for their sins,[137] but the Jews proudly asserted that 'the fire [of hell] will not touch us but for a number of days'.[138] Moreover Jews and Christians claimed that none shall enter Paradise unless he was a Jew or a Christian.[139] Yet at the same time, the Jews claimed that the Christians had nothing, and the Christians said the same about the Jews.[140] When Muhammad spoke to them about Islam, the Jews said: "Our hearts are wrapped" (i.e. they did not hear or understand God's word).[141]

In the face of this arrogance and intransigence, how should the Jews be treated? The Qur'an gives some instructions.

---

[129] 3:93.
[130] 2:104.
[131] 5:43.
[132] 4:153.
[133] 2:104; 4:46.
[134] 5:64, 68.
[135] 9:30.
[136] 5:64.
[137] see 19:71.
[138] 2:80; 3:24.
[139] 2:111.
[140] 2:113.
[141] 2:88.

Part 3: How to treat Jews

Because Jews fall into the category of 'unbelievers' (*kāfirīn*),[142] some of the warnings about unbelievers necessarily apply to the Jews.

(a) Non-Muslims should not be taken as friends/sponsors
Muslims are not allowed to take as friends or sponsors or helpers (*awliyā*)[143] or advisors (*biṭāna*)[144] nor to befriend (*yuwādūn*)[145] non-Muslims (sometimes Jews and Christians are specifically named),[146] unless you fear them.[147] This is because non-Muslims will try to corrupt Muslims[148] and make them reject faith.[149] Only take fellow-Muslims as friends.[150]

(b) Non-Muslims should not be obeyed
Allah forbids Muslims from obeying non-Muslims.[151] Muslims are told: "Believe no-one except the one who follows your religion".[152]

(c) Jews should be challenged about their claims
Since they claimed that the home of the Hereafter with Allah was for them alone among all humanity, then they should be challenged to long for death, if they were truthful. But clearly they would not do so, because their works were inadequate.[153] The Muslims are told to invite them to Islam, and argue with them in the best way.[154]

---

[142] See 2:100; 5:43, 61.

[143] 3:28; 4:89,139,144; 5:80,81; 9:23; 58: 22; 60:1.

[144] 3:118.

[145] 58:22.

[146] 5:51; 58:14; 60:13.

[147] 3:28.

[148] 3:118.

[149] 4:89.

[150] 9:71.

[151] Q.25:52; 26:151; 33:1; 68:8, 10; 76:24.

[152] 3:73.

[153] 2:94.

[154] 16:125.

(d) Muhammad could decide whether or not to arbitrate between them

He was told that if they came to him for a judgement on a dispute, he could either do so in a just way, or decide to turn away from them and refuse to arbitrate, because they already had their own law, the Torah.[155]

(e) Jews (and Christians) should be opposed

They are to be fought against, until they pay the poll-tax (*jizya*) and feel themselves subdued.[156]

Part 4: Judgement on the Jews

The obduracy of the Jews earned them curses from both David and Jesus.[157] They also incurred Allah's curse and wrath.[158] He broke them into various groups on the earth.[159] When they kindled the fire of war, Allah extinguished it,[160] and Allah Himself fought against them.[161] Allah did not wrong them, but they wronged themselves.[162]

But it did not have to be this way. If only the Jews had believed and warded off evil, Allah would have expiated their sins and admitted them to gardens of pleasure.[163] If they had acted according to the Torah, *Injīl* and what had been sent down to them, they would have received provision from above and from below.[164]

But they did not, so Allah does not want to purify their hearts.[165] They were covered with humiliation and misery, and drew on

---

[155] 5:42.
[156] 9:29.
[157] 5:78.
[158] 5:60.
[159] 7:168.
[160] 5:64.
[161] 9:30.
[162] 16:118.
[163] 5:66.
[164] 5:66.
[165] 5:41.

themselves the Wrath of Allah.[166] Allah put enmity and hatred between them until the Day of Resurrection.[167]

Their alienation from Allah had physical ramifications. For their wrongdoing, Allah made unlawful to them certain good foods.[168] In the past, some Jews were transformed into monkeys[169] or pigs and monkeys for their sins,[170] so there is disgrace for them in this world.[171] May their hands be tied, says the Qur'an, and they be accursed for their sayings.[172] They are the worst in rank, and very astray from the right path.[173]

There are eschatological implications for their errors. They, along with Christians, must believe in Jesus before his death, and Jesus will be a witness against them.[174] Allah has cursed them.[175] Christians and Jews are cursed by Allah and also by the cursers.[176] As a result, the Jews will be tormented till the Day of Resurrection,[177] and then there is a great torment for them in the hereafter,[178] because Allah has prepared for them a painful punishment.[179] Their torment will not be lightened.[180] They are the worst of men[181] and they will go to the fire.[182] It is commonly believed that "those on whom is [Allah's] anger"[183] described in the Opening Chapter of the Qur'an (al-fātiḥa) are the Jews.[184]

---

[166] 2:61.

[167] 5:64.

[168] 4:160; 16:118.

[169] 2:65; 7:166.

[170] 5:60.

[171] 5:41.

[172] 5:64.

[173] 5:60.

[174] 4:159.

[175] 4:46, 52.

[176] 2:159.

[177] 7:163, 166-167; 17:104.

[178] 5:41; 3:188.

[179] 4:161.

[180] 2:86.

[181] 98:6.

[182] 3:181; 4:55; 98:6.

[183] 1:7.

[184] e.g. The commentators Jalalayn (http://bit.ly/1MmlKzP) and Ibn Abbas (http://bit.ly/1OjTnjh).

Jews in the Hadith

When we come to the Hadith,[185] we find that the tone is clearly anti-Jewish. At one time, Muhammad stood for a passing Jewish funeral procession,[186] which some scholars claim was a sign of respect.[187] However the scholar Tirmidhi gives a reason for Muhammad standing. Muhammad's grandson Hasan bin Ali reported: "A bier carrying a Jew was brought past when Allah's Messenger (peace be upon him) was sitting in its path, and just *because he did not like having a Jew's bier higher than his head* he stood up."[188] Muhammad later stopped the respectful observance of funerals when he heard this was a Jewish practice. "[H]is practice had been to follow funerals and remain standing until the body was interred. This practice was changed, however, after a rabbi approached him and said: 'We do likewise O Muhammad!' at which point he took his seat, exclaiming 'Oppose them'."[189]

There are nearly 180 references to the Jews in al-Bukhari's Hadith collection, and they are overwhelmingly negative.[190] One account refers to the Jews as "the fools amongst the people".[191] Some Jews, it is claimed, were changed into rats.[192] Muhammad responded to them with double-meaning derogatory greetings.[193]

In the first chapter of the Qur'an, described by Muhammad as the 'greatest'[194] or 'most superior'[195] chapter, or the *umm* ('substance')

---

[185] This section will draw its material from al-Bukhari's hadith collection.

[186] al-Bukhari's hadith (B.x:y = al-Bukhari vol:number) B.2:398, 399.

[187] e.g. Ramadhan, Tariq *The Messenger: The Meanings of the Life of Muhammad,* London: Penguin, 2007 p90.

[188] Transmitted by Tirmidhi no. 521 – italics mine. CD *Islamic Scholar* Hadith/Mishkat.

[189] Seth Ward, "Funerary Practices, Jewish", in Josef W. Meri (ed.) *Medieval Islamic Civilization: an Encyclopedia* 2 vols, New York: Routledge, 2006, vol.1, p269.

[190] The exceptions are (i) the account of a Jewish boy who used to serve the Prophet. When the boy was sick, Muhammad visited him, so the boy embraced Islam (B.2:438; 7:561); (ii) Muhammad exonerated a Jew who had been slapped by a Muslim (B.3:594, 595; 4:620, 626; 6:162; 8:524; 9:52, 564); (iii) Muhammad confirmed a rabbi's assessment of the greatness of God (B.6:335; 9:510, 543, 604) and the earth becoming bread (B.8:527).

[191] B.1:392.

[192] B.4:524.

[193] B.4:186; 8:53, 57, 273, 274, 404, 410; 9:61, 62.

[194] B.6:170.

of the whole Qur'an,[196] and recited compulsorily by Muslims every time they pray,[197] the Jews are labelled as "those who have earned [Allah's] anger."[198] One Jew apparently concurred with this view.[199]

Muhammad made many accusations against the Jews. Muhammad interpreted a dreadful noise after sunset as "the Jews being punished in their graves".[200] Unsurprisingly, the man who worked magic against Muhammad was called "an ally of the Jews",[201] and it was the Jews who tried to poison the Prophet.[202] Gabriel is declared as the enemy of the Jews among the angels.[203]

Muhammad's accusations against the Jews
(B.x:y = al-Bukhari vol:no.)

selling the forbidden fat of animals	B.3:426, 427, 438; 4:666; 6:157
making false oaths	B.3:834; 8:164; 9:36, 37, 302
lying	B.4:546; 5:250
deceiving	B.4:394, 398; 6:91
being insincere	B.5:277
worshipping Ezra as the son of Allah	B.6:105; 9:932.2 c.f. Q.9:30
concealing their scriptures	B.4:829; 6:79; 8:809, 825; 9:633
distorting their scriptures	B.6:12; 9:461
disbelieving their scriptures	B.6:229
disagreeing about their scriptures	B.6:510

The Jews allegedly made unjustified claims, such as "If one has sexual intercourse with his wife from the back, then she will deliver

---

195 B.6:226, 528.

196 B.6:229, 529.

197 B.1:723, 726, 729, 739, 743, 745; 2:419.

198 B.1:749.

199 B.5:169.

200 B.2:45.

201 B.7:660; 8:89.

202 B.7:669.

203 B.5:275; 6:7.

a squint-eyed child,"[204] and it was said that the Jews had bewitched the Muslims so they could have no children.[205] They are blamed for causing meat to decay.[206] They, along with the Christians, are depicted in a story as becoming angry at the generous employer who engaged Muslims late in the day for the same wages.[207] Muhammad prophesies a latter-day genocide in which the rocks betray the Jews by saying: "There is a Jew hiding behind me; so kill him."[208] This Hadith was brought to the attention of the trustees of the University of Southern California, and the Provost ordered that it be removed from the on-line collection of Hadith placed on their server by the Muslim Students Association, since he considered it "despicable".[209]

The Jews are invariably depicted in a bad light. They asked Muhammad difficult questions,[210] and "disapproved" when the *Qibla* was changed from Jerusalem to Mecca.[211] Jews were seen as involved in crime such as cheating on land deals,[212] adultery[213] and murder.[214] Muhammad had to mortgage his armour to a Jew to get credit to buy food,[215] and a Jew refused respite in repayment of a loan, despite Muhammad's intercession.[216] It was Jews who tried to poison the Prophet,[217] for they disbelieved him.[218] Unsurprisingly, the man who worked magic against Muhammad was Labid bin A'sam, a Jew.[219] Gabriel is declared as the enemy of the Jews among the angels.[220]

---

[204] B.6:51.

[205] B.7:378.

[206] B.4:547, 611.

[207] B.3:468, 469, 471; 4:665; 6:539.

[208] B.4:176, 177, 791.

[209] http://www.jihadwatch.org/2008/08/usc-msa-removes-does-not-repudiate-genocidal-Hadith.html, accessed on 9th December, 2009.

[210] B.1:127; 6:245; 9:400, 548, 554.

[211] B.1:39.

[212] B.3:599, 834.

[213] B.2:413; 4:829; 6:79; 8:809, 825; 9:432, 633.

[214] B.3:596; 4:9; 4:398; 7:216.2; 8:164; 9:15, 18, 23, 24, 36, 37, 302.

[215] B.3:282, 283, 309, 404, 453, 454, 571, 690; 4:165; 5:743.

[216] B.3:581, 786; 7:354.

[217] B. 4:394; 7:669.

[218] B.6:252.

[219] B.7:661, 660; 8:89.

[220] B.4:546; 5:275; 6:7.

Every Jew and Christian, it is said, must believe in Jesus before his death, for he will be a witness against them.[221] This statement would have been particularly irksome for the Jews who did not accept Jesus Christ as an authentic prophet.

Muhammad's followers were told not to imitate the Jews in any way. Muslims who go astray are depicted as following the Jews and Christians, even into the holes of sand-lizards,[222] so Muslims are not to copy them. Muslims should dye their grey hair, because Jews and Christians did not.[223] Muslims should not wear false hair, because the Jews did.[224] Muhammad himself initially copied Jewish/Christian hairstyles but later reverted to a pagan coiffure.[225] The Muslim use of the voice for the call to prayer was in contradistinction to the "fire" or "horn" of the Jews and the "bell" of the Christians,[226] as was Friday for the day of prayer instead of Saturday or Sunday.[227] Muslims should not use the same hand gestures in prayer as Jews.[228]

The Prophet clearly wanted to supersede the Jews. When they told him about fasting on the day of Ashura instituted by Moses, Muhammad retorted: "We have more claim over Moses than you," and ordered the Muslims to fast.[229]

His animosity towards the Jews increased. He gave Jews near to Medina an ultimatum: "If you embrace Islam, you will be safe. You should know that the earth belongs to Allah and His Apostle, and I want to expel you from this land. So, if anyone amongst you owns some property, he is permitted to sell it, otherwise you should know that the earth belongs to Allah and His Apostle."[230]

---

[221] B.4:657.

[222] B.4:662; 9:422.

[223] B.4:668; 7:786.

[224] B.4:649; 7:821.

[225] B.7:799 also 5:280.

[226] B.1:577, 578; 4:663.

[227] B.2:1, 21.

[228] B.4:664.

[229] B.3:222; 4:609; 5:279; 6:202, 261.

[230] B.4:392; 9:77, 447.

Eventually Muhammad exiled or executed or enslaved all the Jews from Medina,[231] destroying their farms during a siege.[232] He later invaded the Jewish community of Khaybar making Jews pay yearly 50% of their crops.[233] A Jewish woman had abused and disparaged Muhammad. When a man killed her, the Prophet declared that no recompense was payable for her blood.[234] He sent his men to assassinate the Jews Ka'b bin Ashraf,[235] Abu Rafi[236] and the 120 year old Abu Afak.[237] Muhammad told his followers to "kill any Jew that falls in your power".[238] His enmity towards the Jews never stopped. In "the last moment of his life", Muhammad cursed the Jews and the Christians for building places of worship on the graves of their prophets.[239] The second Caliph 'Umar eventually expelled the Jews from their farms at Khaybar, claiming the Prophet's sanction, and calling them Islam's "enemies".[240]

Conclusion

The Qur'an takes an ambivalent attitude towards the Jewish people.

Some of the 637 verses that relate to the Jews present an affirmative picture. They speak of their privileged status, past salvation history and continuing obligations. The Torah is given many positive ascriptions, paralleling those of the Qur'an itself. Although some verses state that the Jews need not fear or grieve on the Judgement Day, other verses seem to question this. Some of them did assure their salvation by becoming Muslims, but the majority did not.

---

[231] B.5:148, 362.

[232] B.3:519; 4:263; 5:362, 365,366, 406. This destruction of Bani Nadir's date palms is also referred to in Q.59:5.

[233] 1:208, 214, 367, 584, 812; 2:68; 3:405, 437, 485, 521, 524, 527, 531, 657, 678, 881; 4:195; 5:509, 510, 550; 8:169.

[234] Abu Dawud no. 4349.

[235] B.4:271; 3:687; 4:270: 5:369.

[236] B. 5:370, 371.

[237] Ibn Ishaq, *Sirat Rasul Allah*, 675.

[238] Ibn Ishaq, *Sirat Rasul Allah*, 369.

[239] B.1:427, 428; 2:414, 472; 4:660; 5:725, 727; 7:706.

[240] B.3:485, 531, 890; 4:380.

Most of the verses in the Qur'an which describe the Jews take a negative view of them. Their historical disobedience throughout the ages is outlined in great detail. In Muhammad's time they are criticized for mishandling the divine revelation, their greed and violence, their outrageous and untrue statements, and their arrogant attitude towards Allah's messenger.

As a result, they are seen as unbelievers. Consequently Muslims should not take them as friends/sponsors/patrons, nor obey them but instead invite them to Islam and argue with them in the best way. The Jews (and Christians) should also be fought against, and made to pay the poll-tax with submission and humiliation.

There would be a judgement on them because Allah has cursed them. They are the worst of men, and they will go to the fire of hell.

The Hadith's attitude to the Jews is invariably negative. They are criticised for a variety of activities and attitudes: for what they said and what they did. Muhammad told his followers not to imitate them in any way, although he himself did in the earlier stages. His feelings against them increased. Eventually all the Jews in Medina were exiled or executed or enslaved. He attacked and subdued other Jewish communities and individuals, and died cursing Jews and Christians. Claiming Muhammad's sanction, the second Caliph 'Umar exiled all the Jews from the Arabian peninsula.

OUTSIDE INFLUENCES ON JUDAISM[1]

Rich Robinson[2]

The genesis of this paper lies in a question that has arisen in my own circles, namely those of Messianic Jews (Jewish believers in Jesus) and evangelization of the Jewish people. It is the question: does first-century Jewish culture represent a lost ideal? This idea is sometimes expressed in the mistaken notion that the church became hopelessly paganized after the first few centuries and therefore, we are referring to something pure and pristine when we speak of first-century Jewish culture.

The fact, however, is that Judaism and Jewish culture have been influenced for millennia by a host of non-Jewish influences. Jesus and the apostles lived in a society heavily shaped by Hellenism, while later rabbinic Judaism imbibed influences ranging from Aristotelian philosophy to Sufism. There is no "pure" Jewish culture—and there has never been. This fact of history, as it turns out, has accrued to the benefit of the Jewish people, helping ensure their survival and even their flourishing.

The Influence of Hellenistic (Greco-Roman) culture of the 4th-1st centuries BCE

The subject of Hellenistic influence on Judaism has engaged a long roster of Jewish and non-Jewish scholars in the last century or so, including Elias Bickerman, Saul Lieberman, E. R. Goodenough, Morton Smith, S. Stein, Boaz Cohen, Victor Tcherikover, Martin Hengel, David Daube—the list goes on and on. Some of them were maximizers, finding influences of Hellenism everywhere. Others

---

[1] A version of this paper was published in the LCJE Bulletin of the Lausanne Consultation on Jewish Evangelism in 2008.

[2] Richard A. Robinson is a Jewish believer in Jesus. He holds the M.Div. from Trinity Evangelical Divinity School (1978) and the Ph.D. from Westminster Theological Seminary (1993). On staff with Jews for Jesus since 1978, he currently serves as senior researcher at the International Headquarters in San Francisco, CA, USA.

were minimizers and found it hardly at all. It is the good fortune that we now have the book *Judaism and Hellenism in Antiquity* by Lee Levine to summarize the research and give us a balanced picture of state-of-the-art research up to the time of publication in 1999.[3]

What Levine says applies also to the study of earlier and later influences on Judaism, not just those of the 4th to 1st centuries BC. According to Levine, Hellenization was not simply a binary switch, either present or not. Rather, it was a complex process whose description required nuancing. Hellenistic culture could be absorbed deeply in a syncretistic fashion. It could exist as the less extreme level of "synthesis or symbiosis," and at a superficial level, as a kind of decoration as it were. All three levels could occur in society, both in different social groupings and even among people within the same social group.[4]

Levine goes on to consider an older model of cultural influences, whereby outside influence was granted in the case of material culture—food, architecture, that sort of thing, which was considered the "shell"—but not so readily in the religious sphere, the so-called "kernel". That, he says, is hardly an absolute distinction. He continues by outlining the different degrees and types of influence between social classes, geographical areas, rural vs. urban settings, across time, and so forth.

One could substitute "Islamic culture" or other cultural matrices for "Hellenism" and arrive at similar conclusions. For "influences" vary in degree, importance, and nature. Thus even to say that the church was "influenced" by paganism is to say nothing of note unless we talk about how, where, and when—in liturgy? in conception of God's being? in architecture?

What is further important to note is that saying that there was cultural influence is not the same thing as saying there was assimilation, in this case, loss of Jewish identity. Levine explains:

---

[3] Lee I. Levine, *Judaism and Hellenism in Antiquity: Conflict or Confluence?* Peabody, MA: Hendrickson, 1999. See further at David Steinberg, "The Impact of Greek Culture on Normative Judaism from the Hellenistic Period through the Middle Ages," http://www.adath-shalom.ca/greek_influence.htm

[4] Levine, pp21-22.

A conceptual mistake made frequently in the past equates Hellenization and assimilation. To assume a degree of Hellenization has often been construed as the Jews' loss of national or religious identity in favor of something else. **Such a phenomenon, well known in later Jewish history and especially in modern times, was rare in antiquity, at least according to the sources at our disposal. There are very few cases of Jews abandoning their ethnic and religious identity in order to integrate into the larger Greco-Roman society.**[5]

Let us now look at a number of specific areas in which scholars have found Hellenistic influence. As implied above, some of these areas are in material culture, others are more "religious". A listing of many of these areas, loosely arranged on a spectrum from less to more "religious," would include:[6]

1. Coins. In the Persian and early Hellenistic periods (prior to the time of Herod), coins featured symbols from the outside culture, including "the Athenian owl, the Ptolemaic eagle, various human figures, including Ptolemy and his wife, Berenike, an unidentified warrior, a Persian king, a winged deity, perhaps several high priests (Yadua, Yohanan), and a local governor."[7] In Hasmonean times, coins were minted with Greek inscriptions. Notably, in distinction from both earlier and later times, the Hasmoneans did not depict humans or animals on their coins.

2. Burial monuments and graves frequently utilized Greco-Roman architectural motifs.

3. Names. The second generation of Hasmoneans began adopting Greek names.

4. *Commerce.* We find imported wine from Rhodes, for example.

5. Languages. Aramaic ranks first in usage, followed not by Hebrew but by Greek—even in Jerusalem.

6. Governmental practice. The assumption of kingship by the Hasmoneans Aristobulus and Alexander Jannaeus as well as the

---

[5] Levine, pp27-28 (bold added).

[6] The following list benefits greatly from Levine's excellent study.

[7] Levine, p38.

rule of a queen, Salome Alexander, have been traced to Hellenistic models.

7. Urban life.[8] The conversion of Jerusalem *by the Jewish High Priest* into a Hellenistic city about 175 BCE is quite significant. "Jason's move constituted a bold step in the city's adaptation to the wider world, a process which would be interrupted—but only temporarily—by the persecutions of Antiochus IV and the resultant Maccabean revolt."

An important side note here: some have pictured the revolt of the Maccabees as a reaction of "pure" Jews vs. "Hellenized" Jews. However, the Maccabees and their successors the Hasmoneans *were as equally Hellenized as the "Hellenized" Jews.* The Maccabean revolt was not a response to Hellenization but to Antiochus' persecution of Judaism. As just one example of Hellenization among the Hasmoneans, we have only to recall their institution of holidays commemorating military triumphs, such as Nicanor Day (Adar 13)—just as the Greeks did.

Urban life included venues for popular entertainment. In Herodian times, Jerusalem contained a theatre (for music and drama), an amphitheatre (for gladiatorial combat), and a hippodrome (for chariot racing).

8. Literature of the time has been suggested as reflective of Hellenistic genres and ideas.

So far, it may seem that most if not all of this list is more "shell" than "kernel." But then we get to more specifically "religious" customs and institutions, So, in the "religious" area we find:

9. The first fruits (bikkurim) ceremonies of Second Temple Judaism contain elements modeled on pagan culture. "A most striking example," writes Levine, "is the ceremony of bringing the first fruits (*bikkurim*) to Jerusalem. According to the Mishnah, these ceremonies involved a festive procession into the city with the decorated horns of animals, particularly oxen."[9]

---

[8] Levine, p39-40.

[9] Levine, p71.

10. The Sukkot (Feast of Tabernacles) celebrations (which Jesus attended in John 7) likewise contain Greco-Roman elements. One element was the *Simhat Bet Hasho'evah*, the ceremony of drawing water—a first-century water show, if you will. The celebrations "included singing and dancing, juggling and acrobatics, mass processions (often with torches), and carrying items such as willow branches and water libations. All of these activities have striking parallels in contemporary pagan holiday celebrations; clearly some sort of borrowing took place here."[10]

11. The hermeneutical rules–rule of biblical interpretation–used in rabbinic Judaism, such as Hillel's seven rules, likely trace back to Greco-Roman models.[11]

13. The ketubah (Jewish wedding contract), which was acknowledged as an innovation by the rabbis, may have derived from Hellenistic Egyptian models.[12]

14. The Passover Seder likely derived from a Greco-Roman institution known as the symposium, as proposed by S. Stein, who suggested that the following well-known *Seder* elements had origins in Hellenistic institutions: "questions about food at the outset of the evening; the types of food eaten before the meal (greens, apples and nuts mixed with wine); a cup of wine to initiate the evening, followed by others; a description of those in attendance at a particular symposium; a midrash referring to a classical text, around which much of the discussion focused; and concluding hymns of praise to the god or king to whom the evening was dedicated. The custom of reclining while eating is another practice at the *Seder* that is clearly of Greco-Roman origin."[13]

15. Synagogue art ranged from traditional Jewish motifs such as the menorah, to the rather startling and widespread use of the zodiac. It is not clear if in these cases the zodiac represents just an artistic decorative motif or reflects some underlying theological idea.[14]

---

[10] Levine, pp71-72.

[11] Levine, pp115-16.

[12] Levine, pp116-19.

[13] Levine, p121.

[14] Levine, pp152-53.

16. Synagogue liturgy[15]. Some suggest that communal prayer, and specific prayers such as the *Shema* and the *Amidah* (which today remain core components of synagogue services) were influenced by Hellenistic models.

Crucially, at this early period we learn that adoption of outside culture helped Jewish survival. This cannot be stressed strongly enough. Levine cites Elias Bickerman, who "has aptly remarked with regard to Hellenistic native rulers who took over in the wake of the Seleucid collapse: 'Cosmopolitanism was the price of independence.'"[16]

To sum up so far: Jewish life, religious or not, was influenced in various degrees by Hellenistic, Greco-Roman culture. The examples given do not seem to impinge on the foundations of Jewish faith—that there is one God, and that his Torah should be followed. We have not even touched on things such as theology proper: the person of God, the messianic hope, and so on, and how Hellenistic influence may have affected those notions or later ideas such as the concept of an oral law, one of the foundations of rabbinic Judaism.

But we have seen enough to ask questions such as these: Is the *seder* authentically Jewish? Is the *Amidah* prayer? For that matter, is Second-Temple Judaism authentically Jewish? One cannot simply say that Second Temple Judaism is not "Old Testament Judaism," which never existed in any "pure," standardized, authoritative form either. To be sure, the Torah was the standard, but the cultural forms it was expressed in were never purely uniform. The culture of Moses' day was not that of Solomon's. Culture is complex. There is no ground for asserting a kind of "purity" to first-century or any other form of Judaism. If we learn anything, it is that Jesus and the apostles were part and parcel of their era. If there is a shell and a kernel to be had, it would be better to think of the kernel as the transcultural biblical/gospel message and the shell as its expression.

---

[15] Levine, pp164-66.
[16] Levine, pp45-46.

The Influence of Greek Philosophy on Rabbinic Judaism in the medieval period

Greek influence continued in later times, albeit in a different direction. It was the medieval Jewish philosopher Moses Maimonides (1135–1204), and others too, who believed that Greek philosophy and the Hebrew Bible could be harmonized. His discussion of the nature of God relies heavily upon Aristotelian thought in interaction with the system of Islamic philosophy called *Kalam*, the latter of which, however, he rejected.

> "Maimonides sought to bridge [earlier] interpretations with his assertion that the unity of God is unique... Maimonides suggested that the intrinsic unity of God should be conceived as radically different in character from the unity of a species that is composed of discrete members, or from the unity of an organism that is made up of interrelated yet relatively distinct elements."[17]

Modern Rabbinic Judaism's view of God's unity owes more to Aristotle than most Jews realize. Such a view differs substantially from the conceptions of the divine that we find in earlier Judaism, which as Benjamin Sommer has recently, shown allowed for fluidity and multiplicity in conceptions of God's nature.[18] (Sommer in fact argues that the Trinity and Incarnation are not what really separate Judaism and Christianity, but rather such factors as the conception of the Messiah.) However that may be, Maimonides, under Aristotelian influence, laid the groundwork for the "unitary" view of God's nature that characterizes Judaism today, in which God is "one," with no space left for conceiving him as, e.g., "three in one."

It should be noted that both the earlier Hellenistic and the medieval Aristotelian influences continue to inform Judaism up to the present day.

Islamic Influences (approximately 950-1150A.D.)

It is unfortunate that an important book on this subject—*Islamic Influences on Jewish Worship* by Naphtali Wieder, published in

---

[17] Martin Sicker, *Between Man and God: Issues in Judaic Thought*, Westport, CT: Greenwood Press, 2002, p51. See also Kenneth Seeskin, ed., *The Cambridge Companion to Maimonides*, Cambridge; New York: Cambridge University Press, 2005, pp83ff.

[18] Benjamin D. Sommer, *The Bodies of God and the World of Ancient Israel*, New York: Cambridge University Press, 2009.

1947—is only available in Hebrew. However, an English-language article concerning Wieder's book, by Shalom Goldman of Emory University, appeared in 1999.[19]

Goldman's article provides a brief but positive appraisal. At one time, scholarly consensus postulated Jewish (and Christian) influence on Islam; in recent times many agree that the influences go in the other direction also. (Cultural influences are rarely if ever a one-way street.) Wieder's discussion concerns nine rituals associated with prayer, including ablutions before praying and the direction the congregation must face. While Maimonides recommended changes in liturgy in reaction against Islam, his son Abraham found value in adopting certain Islamic practices.

In connection with Abraham Maimonides, we should mention that the mystical stream of Islam known as Sufism shows points of mutual influence with medieval Judaism and *kabbalah* (Jewish mysticism). Paul Fenton writes about Abraham:

> ... he was also an ardent protagonist of the Sufi form of Jewish pietism henceforth known as *hasidut* ... Abraham Maimonides composed a commentary on the Pentateuch wherein he often depicts the ancient biblical characters as pietists in the same way as Sufi literature adorns the Prophet [Muhammad] and his companions in the garb of the early Sufis.[20]

Abraham regarded the Sufi garments and Sufi initiation rituals as originating with the prophets of Israel. Sufi self-mortification and sleep deprivation, he said, may have originated with King David![21] If this is not scientific evidence of influence, it certainly demonstrates a lively conversation and an *openness* to whatever real influences lay at hand.

And these real influences shaped the development of medieval Jewish life, especially during the "Golden Age of Spanish Jewry." Contact with the Muslim world encouraged Jewish exploration in

---

[19] Shalom Goldman, "An Appraisal of Naphtali Wieder's 'Islamic Influences on Jewish Worship' on the Fiftieth Anniversary of Its Publication", *Medieval Encounters* 5, 1999, pp11-16.

[20] Paul B. Fenton, "Judaism and Sufism," ch. 10 in Daniel H. Frank and Oliver Leaman, *The Cambridge Companion to Medieval Jewish Philosophy*, Cambridge University Press, 2003; p207.

[21] Fenton, p208.

mathematics, medicine and astronomy. Moreover, Arabic, not Hebrew or Aramaic, became the language of the common people, and also of many of the great medieval Jewish philosophers and grammarians.

> "In the literature of philosophy and even of theology one may say without hesitation that the influence flowed from Islam to Judaism and not the other way around. The notion of a theology, of a formulation of religious belief in the form of philosophical principles, was alien to the Jews of Biblical and Talmudic times."[22]

In other words, not only the content of Jewish theology, such as the nature of God's unity, was altered under outside influence, but the *way* theology was done, *how* Jews thought about theology, was affected by currents in the Islamic world.

Influences from Christianity

Elements of the synagogue liturgy—such as the *piyyutim*, a genre of prayer which first arose in Jewish worship in the 4th–5th c. A.D.—seem to have been adopted from Christian practice of the Byzantine period. (On the other hand, the centrality of Torah reading and study appears to have moved from synagogue to church).[23]

> There are several powerful arguments for assuming Jewish adoption and adaptation of such an outside model: this liturgical form appeared in the synagogue context soon after its introduction into the church; the Hebrew terms have exact equivalents in Greek (piyyut deriving from *poema* or *poesis*, and paytan [piyyut composer] from *poetes*); similar stylistic principles appear in both Hebrew and Greek versions; and this new practice was one of many instances of Jewish borrowing of church architectural, artistic, and even epigraphical forms.[24]

---

[22] Bernard Lewis, *The Jews of Islam,* Princeton, NJ: Princeton University Press, 1987, p80.

[23] Levine, pp163-64.

[24] Levine, p164.

Some ground-breaking if controversial work has been done for this period by Israeli scholar Israel J. Yuval.[25] At the outset he tells us one of his presuppositions:

> ...there follows another basic assumption of this book: that whenever we find a similarity between Judaism and Christianity, and we do not have grounds to suggest a shared heritage, we may assume that it is indicative of the influence of the Christian milieu on the Jews, and not vice versa, unless it may be proved that the Jewish sources are more ancient. The reason for this assumption is quite simple: minority cultures tend to adopt the agenda of the majority culture.[26]

This influence was sometimes "negative"; that is, Judaism developed in conscious opposition to Christian ideas. For example, we have the concept in rabbinic Judaism of the Oral Law, mentioned above; i.e., the idea that along with the written Law delivered to Israel on Mount Sinai, the inspired interpretation of that Law was given as well, to be ultimately compiled in the Mishnah and Talmud. We cannot here explore whether any Hellenistic influences were at work in the development of this conception, but according to Yuval, there clearly was Christian influence: "The Oral Torah," he writes, "is, in the deepest sense, a Jewish answer to the Christian Torah, the New Testament."[27] This, at least, is the view of a later midrash, or homily:

> This is the explanation of the following passage from *Midrash Tanhuma* (*Ki Tisa*, sec. 34): "The Holy One blessed be He said to the nations [i.e., the Christians]: 'You say that you are My sons? Know, that only he with whom my *mysterion* is to be found is my son. And what is that? This is the Mishnah, that was given verbally.'" Bergman noted that the term *mysterion* is intended to refute Paul's argument that the Christian gospel is the mystery (Eph 6:19). See M. Bergman, "The Scales are not 'Even'" [in Hebrew], *Tarbiz* 53 (1984): 289-92, esp. 291 n. 14a.[28]

Whether that was an after-the-fact explanation or not, Judaism here appears to have developed in a negative dialectic with Christianity.

---

[25] For example, I. J. Yuval, *Two Nations in Your Womb: Perceptions of Jews and Christians in Late Antiquity and the Middle Ages*, translated from Hebrew by B. Harshav and J. Chipman, Berkeley: University of California Press, 2006.

[26] Yuval, pp21-22.

[27] Yuval, p90.

[28] Yuval, p90 n. 140.

A similar development is seen in the rituals of the *Seder* such as the *afikoman* [29] and the order of elements in the *Seder*:

> In light of all this, the answer to the wise son (or the foolish son, in the Palestinian Talmud) assumes new meaning, including the quotation from *m. Pes.* 10.5: "One does not add an *afikoman* after the Passover feast." To understand its full significance, we need to examine Melito's use of the word *aphikomenos* (which means coming or arriving) to describe Jesus's incarnation, his appearance on earth, and his Passion: "He who, coming from heaven to the earth" (*Houtos aphikomenos ex ouranon epi ten gen.*) Melito's remarks about Jesus's *afikoman* and his suffering on earth appear immediately after his homily on the Passover sacrifice as a symbol of Jesus, and thus presenting an entire homily on the Christological meaning of the Paschal offering, the matzah, and the bitter herbs—a parallel to Rabban Gamaliel's homily. In light of that the rule that "one does not add an *afikoman* after the Passover feast" was chosen as the answer to the wise son in order to pull out the rug from under the Christian interpretation. The confrontation of the Talmudic Sages with the Christian interpretation of the ceremonies performed at the Passover feast is consistent with another change concerning the order of the meal made in the early amoraic [30] period. During the period of the Mishnah, the meal preceded the Haggadah [31], while in the amoraic period it became customary to read the Haggadah before the meal; David Daube has already suggested that this change was also intended to oppose the Christian interpretation of the holiday feast and its symbols. [32]

What we are dealing with is essentially a counter-story developed under the influence of Christianity. But Yuval takes care to balance the "negative" counter-story approach with a more positive one:

> Yet not every ceremony, even if it exists in a polemical environment, is necessarily polemical. Its function may be specifically to internalize the language of the opponent, as in the case of the *afikoman*, by "Judaizing" the Host. In a similar vein,

---

[29] Ed: The *afikoman* is a half-piece of matzo which is broken in two during the early stages of the Passover *Seder* and set aside to be eaten as a dessert after the meal.

[30] Ed: The Amora were a group of Rabbis (about 200-500CE) who discussed the Mishnaic Law and whose discussions are recorded in the Talmud.

[31] Ed: The Haggadah is a Jewish text that sets forth the order of the Passover *Seder*.
[32] Yuval, pp76-77.

Ivan Marcus has recently noted a similar phenomenon in his book about the ceremony of bringing a child to school, which included eating cookies in the shapes of the letters of the alphabet, smeared with honey. Marcus notes parallels in terms of the visual and thematic similarity between eating the letters of the Torah, the Corpus Dei in Jewish eyes, and eating the Host, the Corpus Christi for Christians.[33]

Conclusion

In all the examples we have discussed, cultural borrowing was not to the exclusion of Judaism; we are not talking about assimilation but a realignment, so to speak, of Jewish identity. As we have said, cultural adoption and adaptation helped ensure Jewish survival.

Similarly, the interplay between rabbinic Judaism and Greek philosophy, Islam and Christianity helped Judaism to survive and flourish in environments that otherwise could have overwhelmed the Jewish people. This remains true of contemporary Jewish adoptions and adaptations of Western culture, but that will be a topic for another time.

---

[33] Yuval, pp247-48.

FROM EASTERN RELIGIONS TO NEW AGE RELIGION IN THE WEST[1]

Paul Rawson[2]

Introduction

New Age Religion has gradually seeped into Western culture and public discourse. Speaking after his victory in the 2016 Australian Tennis Open, Novak Djokovic's reluctance to place himself above his opponents in ability was expressed with distinct New Age resonance:

> "I don't want to allow myself to be in that frame of mind. Because if I do, a person becomes too arrogant and thinks that he's a higher being or better than everybody else. You can get a big slap from karma very soon. I don't want that."[3]

Much of the growth in New Age Religion has been during the past 50 years, largely due to the expansion and influence of eastern religions in the Western world. From the mid to late 20th century as immigration has increased in volume between the East and West, many have explored the practices and beliefs of these religions with Eastern roots, such as Buddhism and Hinduism. Many in the West, disillusioned with the church, were search for a new set of beliefs and teachings to follow. This has gradually evolved into 'New Age Religion', which encompasses the universalism and relativism of Eastern religions, and also incorporates many of their practices.

---

[1] Ed: This paper should be read in conjunction with the following papers by Michelle Stevens and Kate Lim.

[2] Paul Rawson currently serves as an Elder at City on a Hill Geelong while working full-time in the IT industry. He is a final year Masters of Divinity student at Reformed Theological College. Paul became a Christian after a surprising journey from atheist to seeker to evangelist.

[3] http://www.firstpost.com/sports/dont-want-a-big-slap-from-karma-australian-open-champ-djokovic-stays-grounded-after-record-2606014.html

What is 'New Age Religion'?

While New Age Religion is the product of many different doctrinal systems, it has become an umbrella term for a large collection of different beliefs, values and practices. In his assessment of the New Age, Phillip Seddon describes it as "a spaghetti junction, an extraordinary farrago of ideas, a whole phalanx of inter-connected fronts."[4] In other words, it is essentially a "feel-good" religion, in which individuals choose to believe what they would like to believe, based on the universal assumption that all paths lead to God. Although few would tick the "New Age Religion" box on the census form, New Age Religion has infiltrated our societies, values, and practices. Harold Netland, in *Encountering Religious Pluralism* says that "By the 1990's the symbols of Hindu, Buddhist and Taoist spirituality were so prevalent that it was increasingly difficult to distinguish the east from the west."[5] Since then, it has become deeply ingrained in Western Culture. The aim of this paper is to address the extent to which New Age Religion reflects the influence of Eastern religions in the West.

Firstly, it is important to note some of the distinguishing features of New Age Religion. Daren Kemp says that "On the one hand, the New Age-generated huna[6] presents itself as something very special and particular, but at the same time, the universality of beliefs and techniques that it entails are stressed."[7] The teachings and practices of the New Age are both very broad and very specific. New Age is represented in various practices, most of which have a focus on spirituality: meditation, yoga, Tantra, Chinese medicine, tarot cards, astrology and psychic readings. The general belief behind such practices is that holistic spiritual development will improve one's *karma*, an idea that has ancient roots in Eastern religions.

What is Eastern Religion?

There are many organised belief systems that can fall under the banner of Eastern religions, but for the purposes of this paper, we

---

[4] Phillip Seddon, *The New Age – An Assessment*, Nottingham: Grove Books Limited,1990, p4.
[5] Harold Netland, *Encountering Religious Pluralism*, Downers Grove, Il., InterVarsity Press, 2001, p106.
[6] *Huna* is a Hawaiian word used to describe the New Age Movement.
[7] Daren Kemp, James R. Lewis, *Handbook of New Age*, Leiden: Brill, 2007, p326.

will focus on the two most prominent faiths in this category: Hinduism and Buddhism. We will consider how these, in particular, have influenced the growth of New Age Religion in the West.

Of these two religions Hinduism is the much older religion, and in some ways is the parent of Buddhism.[8] Chandler's comment on the influence of both these religions in regards to New Age Western beliefs is:

> Buddhism like other major world religions is not one monolithic system of belief and practice; neither, of course is the New Age philosophy. But Buddhism's influence on New Age thinking is indisputable. So is that of Buddhism's parent religion, Hinduism, which predates Buddhism by at least a thousand years.[9]

Hinduism and Buddhism

Hinduism is a very broad term that encompasses a broad range of beliefs and denotes the religion of the majority of people in India and Nepal, and of some minority communities in other regions, such as the Hindu Balinese of Indonesia. Hinduism is extremely diverse and its history long and complex.[10] This vastness and all-inclusiveness is one of the principles that has seeped into the New Age Religion, in that it accepts all beliefs. Tolerance and respect is at the heart of both Hinduism and New Age Religion. Much of the Vedic textual material has been used by gurus as they have taught internationally on spirituality and well-being.

Buddhism developed in approximately 500BC when Buddha lived, and developed his teachings. Peter Harvey writes

> The English term 'Buddhism' correctly indicates that the religion is characterized by a devotion to 'the Buddha', 'Buddhas or 'buddha-hood'. 'Buddha' is not a proper name, but a descriptive title meaning 'Awakened One' or 'Enlightened One'[11]

---

[8] Ed: See Elizabeth Greentree's article in this present volume.

[9] Chandler, p44.

[10] Gavin D Flood, *An Introduction to Hinduism*, Cambridge: Cambridge University Press, 1996, p5.

[11] Peter Harvey, *An Introduction to Buddhism: Teachings, History and Practices*, Cambridge: Cambridge University Press, 2012, p1.

Buddhism in itself is not an exclusive religion, but is a set of teachings that can accompany and support other belief structures, if so desired. As Buddhist teachings have spread in the West, they have been varyingly received, with most followers choosing to adopt some, but not necessarily all, of the Buddha's teachings. This has led to the practice within New Age Religion of picking up beliefs that suit the follower, and provide good *karma*.

Age of Postmodernity

To properly grasp the growth of New Age Religion in the West, we need to understand the period in which it came into existence. Most commentators agree that New Age Religion grew rapidly in the West between the 1970's and the late 1990's. In the 1970's, Western societies were marked by late industrialisation, rationalism and a rapid process of secularisation. People increasingly questioned traditions, established systems and religions. Many people left the church. It was the age of postmodernism, which some have described as 'hyper-modernity' or 'ultra-modernity'.[12] Postmodernism rejects absolute truths, and frees people to believe what they want, how they want, when they want. Stanley J Grenz summarises postmodernism well when he says that 'It asserts that the world has no centre, only differing viewpoints and perspectives.'[13]

In the age of postmodernism, the cultural setting of the West was ripe for the expansion of Eastern Religions. Many people were leaving churches, and were looking for what they perceived as more accepting, tolerant, beliefs that seemed to fit the mood of the times. A radical self-centeredness became part of the nature of New Age Spirituality with a focus on self, self-improvement, and, self-realisation. By this stage there were already many resources from the Eastern Religions widely available in the Western world.

The Expansion of Eastern Religions

---

[12] Millard J, Erickson, *Postmodernizing The Faith,* Grand Rapids, MI: Baker Books, 1998, p50.

[13] Stanley J Grenz, *A Primer on Postmodernism,* Cambridge, MA: William B Eerdmans Publishing Company, 1996, p7.

Even as far back as 1879, foundations were being laid for the influence of Buddhism in the West. Carl Jackson, noting the reception that welcomed a poem on the life of Buddha, 'The Light of Asia', says:

> Enthusiastically reviewed and widely quoted, hotly attacked and passionately defended, perhaps no work on Buddhism has ever approached its popular success. Certainly no event in the late nineteenth century did more to rivet attention on Buddhism.[14]

Netland also notes that by the mid 1990's, there were already many translations of Hindu and Buddhist texts throughout the Western world.[15] This facilitated Westerners who were searching for a new identity, as they could pick up ideas and concepts from these Eastern Religions. Between 1966 and 2001, the Australian Census recorded a decline in Christianity as a proportion of Australia's population from 88.2% to 68%.[16] Some of those who left Christianity, no doubt, adopted the teachings of New Age Religion. Netland also notes that "Although New Agers reject much of institutional, traditional religion (they are into "spirituality" not "religion"), they unashamedly draw upon ancient religious traditions, whether Hindu, Buddhist or shamanic."[17] So especially throughout the 1970's and 1980's, New Age Religion developed through the spreading of resources, travel of westerners to places of Eastern Religions, and through the travel of gurus from India to western countries.

As an example, Richard Alpert grew up in America as an atheist, and as a young man was searching for purpose and identity, so he travelled to India in 1967. There, Alpert found his own personal guru, which transformed his life. Alpert subsequently returned to America, changed his name, and became a public teacher and proclaimer of the New Age Religion. The Beatles also had a strong influence in the expansion of Eastern religions into the West and the establishment of New Age thinking as a visible religious choice.

---

[14] Carl T Jackson, *The Oriental Religions and American Thought: Nineteenth-Century Explorations*, Westport, CT: Greenwood, 1981, p143.

[15] Netland, p107.

[16] *Year Book Australia*, 2006, Australian Bureau of Statistics.
http://www.abs.gov.au/ausstats/abs@.nsf/46d1bc47ac9d0c7bca256c470025ff87/bfdda1c
a506d6cfaca2570de0014496e!OpenDocument, cited on 30/05/2014

[17] Netland, p109.

In particular, George Harrison, who was raised a Roman Catholic, became interested in Hinduism. It was after their visit to India in 1968, in which they attended a Transcendental Meditation training session taught by Maharishi Mahesh Yogi, that the Beatles' passion for and growth in spirituality started to permeate their music and the pop-culture scene.

The influence of Gurus

Of course, it wasn't just Westerners proclaiming these new ideas. There were also many gurus from India and beyond who travelled through Western countries teaching their relative spiritualties. In *Understanding the New Age,* Chandler wrote a chapter on 'Gifted Gurus', in which he outlines the significant impact Hindu gurus and Buddhist monks had on public thought throughout the 1970's and 1980's. These gurus and monks included Baba Ram Dass, Swami Muktananda and Guru Maharaj Ji. Much of their teaching was about self-worth and holistic healings, which appealed to many people who were against the more traditional teachings of the church. As Duncan Ferguson notes:

> in the 60's, 70's, 80's there was the perception that the traditional forms of Christian orthodoxy were shopworm, exclusive, or just plain irrelevant. ... And here was the opportunity for authentic experiential entrance into the world of intimacy, ultimacy, and identity through discipline and practice that the Eastern traditions at their best offer.[18]

Even the term "guru", which was traditionally used by Hindu or Buddhist teachers from the East, has now been widely used in the West. David Smith writes:

> The term guru, as all-knowing personal guide in a particular discipline, or in respect of life in general, has been readily adopted in the West.[19]

Smith goes on to comment about how modernity was and is a very profitable place for gurus:

---

[18] Duncan S. Ferguson, *New Age Spirituality An Assessment,* Louisville: John Knox Press, 1993, p64.

[19] David Smith, *Hinduism and Modernity,* Malden: John Wiley & Sons, 2008, p179.

For the guru, modernity can be a profitable home, encouraging his entrepreneurship, spreading his ideas more easily, fostering innovation in techniques and doctrine. From the point of view of traditional Hinduism, gurus are generally maintaining traditional spirituality, but packaging it attractively for the modern world, and also spreading it beyond the shores of India. They are living exponents of the truths of Hinduism.[20]

It is not difficult to visualise how Eastern Religions took advantage of a decline in numbers for Christianity and the many people that were searching for new teachings and beliefs. The gurus were very efficient at spreading their teaching. How much of their teaching has remained as part of the New Age Religion?

Evidence of Eastern Religions in modern-day 'New Age Religion'

Certainly the influence of New Age Religion is visible throughout Western societies today. Chandler comments:

New Age influence has indeed touched every facet of contemporary life. Its popularisers and their beliefs are often visible on your television set, at the movies, in printed horoscopes, or at your local health-food store. Even sports and exercise programs, motivational training, psychological counselling, and religious classes are frequent pipelines for New Age thinking.[21]

As we consider certain practices in New Age Religion, we can see clear links to the practices of ancient Eastern Religions. For example, Yoga is practiced by people all over the world, from all different backgrounds, races, and religions. Although it is commonly thought of as part of the New Age Religion, its roots lie in Hinduism.

Other examples demonstrating the evolution of New Age Religion from Eastern religions include fortune telling; horoscope reading; a growing emphasis on meditation; body, mind and spirit festivals; a focus on angels and the use of crystals. Many of these practices are

---

[20] Smith, p180.
[21] Chandler, p20.

now commonplace in Western society, and suggest significant shaping of modern Western culture by the East. This process was already well-established in the 1970s; in a 1978 Gallup Poll 10 million Americans said that they were involved in some aspect of Eastern mysticism.[22]

Popular Hollywood star Oprah Winfrey is an example of someone who promotes New Age Religion,[23] without necessarily realising the ancient origins of the teachings. Much of what Winfrey teaches is that "all paths lead to God" and that life is a process of improving ourselves holistically, thus improving our karma. Even on the topic of suffering Oprah has adopted a lot of her beliefs from Buddhist teaching. Jennifer Harris, in her book *The Oprah Phenomenon*, says that "Oprah's New Age world answered the question of suffering. Individuals would experience varying degrees of pain based on their karma and their intentions in the face of accumulated karma".[24]

Conclusion

Although New Age does derive its teachings from multiple sources, it is clear that the main doctrines of New Age Religion have developed from the increasing influence of Eastern Religions on Western thinking. Eastern Religions are no longer distant ideas or concepts, but are now ingrained in Western society. This is partly a result of the age of postmodernism, which witnessed a large group of people leaving the church and turning to the resources of Eastern Religions, and listening to teachings of travelling gurus from Eastern backgrounds.

---

[22] Chandler, p21.

[23] Harris Jennifer, *The Oprah Phenomenon*, Lexington: University of Kentucky Press, 2007, p133.

[24] Harris, p136.

PART TWO:

CHRISTIAN RESPONSES

HINDUISM, CHRISTIANITY AND KARMA:
a Christian Response

Michelle Stevens[1]

Origin and core beliefs of Hinduism

Hinduism is one of the world's oldest living religions. It began in India, where it has had a significant role in shaping culture and family practices.[2] Hinduism is more correctly defined as a mix of many 'Hindu' faiths and traditions, which have been grouped together in the umbrella term 'Hinduism'.[3] The term Hinduism[4] was created by the British in the 19th century to distinguish all non-Islamic people in India, and as such doesn't always clearly refer to those who follow the 'Hindu religion'.[5] However, we do know the Hindu faith began as a Vedic religion based on revelations to ancient seers, and so is unique in that it has no known human founders.[6] This religion is represented by over 900 million Hindus, the majority living in India, but now practiced over the world.[7]

A complex religion to understand, Alamu describes Hinduism as:

> a religion with many "no's". No founder, no definite creed, no priestly hierarchy, no single universally accepted scripture, no

---

[1] Michelle Stevens works as the Associate Pastor overseeing Generations at Clovercrest Baptist Church in Adelaide. She previously worked as a Physiotherapist before following God's call to undertake graduate studies in theology at MST. After completing a Graduate Diploma in Divinity, she is now working on her Masters. Michelle is married to Mike Stevens and together they have three children.

[2] Akiti Glory Alamu, 'The Concept of Karma in Hinduism and Christianity: An Appraisal', *Asia Journal of Theology* 23/2, 2009, p245-246.

[3] M. Baumann, 'Hinduism', in *Religions of the World,* ed. J. Melton & M Baumann, Denver and Oxford: ABC-CLIO, 2002, p586.

[4] Ed: The word 'Hindu', however, is much older and is derived through Persian from the Sanskrit word 'Sindhu'.

[5] Baumann, p586.

[6] Baumann, p588.

[7] Alamu, p246 & Cybelle Shattuck, *Hinduism,* London: Routledge, 1999, p102.

single moral code or theological system, no clearly defined way of salvation and no single concept of god central to it, no conversion and no missionary enterprise.[8]

Hinduism actually appears as more of a philosophy than a religion. With over 330 million gods which can be worshipped and such diversity it makes Christian witnessing a challenge.[9] This is confounded by the fact that the Hinduism of India is both a way of life and a national religion, whereas the Hinduism practiced in the West can be expressed quite differently.[10]

Despite this complexity we do see some core beliefs and practices shared by the diverse expressions of the Hindu faith:[11]

Atman-Brahman – Hindus believe in the doctrine of the *Atman-Brahman*. There is an uncreated, eternal being, which controls all – the *Brahman*. Within each human is an *atman*, or soul, which is a part of the *Brahman* and once liberated will return to the *Brahman*.[12]

Samsara – this is known as the never ending wheel of rebirth[13] 'a cyclic process with no clear beginning or end that encompasses lives of perpetual, serial attachments'.[14]

Dharma – is the duty or obligation which a person must fulfil, which is dependent on their birth.[15]

Karma – is understood as one's actions and the cause and effect that determines the rebirth cycle. Actions, if they are free from

---

[8] Alamu, pp246-247.

[9] Rodney Peavy, *Way of Life: Evangelism for Hindus.*
http://burningbones.com/web_documents/way_of_life_-_evangelism_for_hidus.pdf, cited 14 Jan, 2011.

[10] Alamu, p246.

[11] Baumann, p593.

[12] Hinduism, *Britannica Encyclopaedia of World Religions,* Chicago: Encyclopaedia Britannica, 2006, p437 & Baumann, p593.

[13] Baumann, p593.

[14] BEWR, p438.

[15] Baumann, p593 & Winfried Corduan, *Beyond Karma: Sin in Hinduism*
http://www.wincorduan.net/Beyond%20Karma.pdf, cited 8 Jan 2010.

desire, create good *karma*, or if driven by desire result in bad *Karma* and a constant cycle of rebirth.[16]

Varna – is the status or caste system whereby groups are organised and hierarchy exists. *Varna* is organised by birth, family groups, heritage and social status. It is thought that a lower social status is due to bad *karma* from a former life.[17]

Moksha – the eventual liberation from the cycle; the final destination and escape.[18]

Sacred Writings – there are two main types of sacred writings that are accepted: the sacred *Sruti*, which include the *Rig Veda* and *Upanishads*; and the *Smriti*, the traditions, stories and epics such as the *Bhagavad Gita*.[19]

As Hinduism spreads and traditional religion adapts some variations occur. The common elements still seen in practice appear to be the authority of the Vedic Scriptures, worship of deities, significance of the epics, assumption of reincarnation and with it *karma* and a recognized Indian heritage.[20]

Some comparisons between Hinduism and Christianity

When comparing Hinduism and Christianity we see many differences. The Hindu belief in god affirms the existence of a god, an eternal Brahman that exists in all, a spark of divinity found in everything.[21] However Hindu worship of god is not necessarily tied to a definite being; instead there may be many 'gods' in nature and character.[22] The Christian belief is in direct contrast to this: there is only one God (Deut 6:4), and no others are to be worshipped (Ex

---

[16] BEWR, p438 & Baumann, p593.

[17] BEWR, p459.

[18] BEWR, p438 & Baumann, p593.

[19] Rodney Peavy, *Way of Life: Evangelism for Hindus*, www.burningbones.com/web_documents/way_of_life_-_evangelism_for_hindus.pdf (14 Jan, 2011), cited 21 Feb 2014.

[20] David Burnett, *The Spirit of Hinduism*, Oxford & Grand Rapids: Monarch Books, 2006, p283.

[21] Ian Benson, *Evangelising Hindus and Buddhists*, Shropshire: The Missionary Training Service, 1998, pp12-13.

[22] Alamu, p246.

20:3). Hindus believe in god as a distant concept controlling everything, and use other gods to ask for help when needed.[23] In contrast Christians know God as the one, almighty yet personal God, who is intimately involved with His people (Ps 50:15, Ps 139:13). [24]

Within the Hindu understanding of god, there exists an acceptance of the three parts to *Saguna Brahman* (Brahman with attributes): Brahma, Vishnu and Shiva. Although some may conclude similarities to the Christian Trinity, the difference is that the Christian Trinity is in fact one God (John 14:9-17), whereas Hindus worship any one of the three.[25]

The belief in a soul exists in both Hindu and Christian thought. However Christian belief is that a soul is created by God for a relationship with God (Gen 1:27). This does not correlate with the Hindu idea that a soul, once liberated, goes back to become one with and part of the Brahman.[26]

Samsara refers to the ongoing cycle of rebirth whereas Christians believe in a 'new birth' in Christ (2 Cor 5:17) resulting in rest and eternal afterlife (John 3:16, Heb 4:9-11). The *moksha* that Christians speak of is salvation and eternal life in Heaven (John 3:16), not a return to oneness with the *Brahman*.

Dharma speaks of duty and obligation, Christians too have a sense of duty and calling (Matt 28:20); however service is out of a relationship with and love for God. There is no sense that duty will save, but instead grace is the key (Eph 2:8-9). This grace is open to all, not limited to any particular caste. All are equal in Christ; there is no *varna* in the eyes of Jesus (Gal 3:28).

Karma

Karma is defined as '[t]he Sanskrit term meaning "action"'; that is, it is the accumulations of one's actions over one's lifetime. 'Upon

---

[23] Benson, p14-15.

[24] Benson, pp12-13.

[25] S. Kulandran, *Grace in Christianity and Hinduism,* London:Billing & Sons Limited, 1964, p145.

[26] BEWR, p437.

death, an individual's *karma* – this store of the results of actions – determines whether one is reborn in a higher or lower status'.[27]

Karma can also refer to that 'action' or 'duty' which particularly relates to caste and obligations under which a person operates.[28] It is also associated with Vedic practices and spoken of in the Vedic texts as a ritual action, a rite to be performed. Rites and practices could involve evil practices such as black magic, or good ones such as completing a prescribed rite. Correct performance of the prescribed rite would result in reaching heaven.[29]

The *Rig Veda* speaks of *karma* as duties, obligations, works or actions: a 'non-*samsara*' meaning of *karma*.[30] This definition of *karma* as action continued and coincided with a developed idea of cause and effect. The understanding grew that 'action' became the cause of certain consequences.[31]

In the *Upanishadic* tradition the theory of *karma* developed from a ritual idea into a moral issue.[32] *Brhad Aranyaka Upanishad* states, 'one becomes good by good action, bad by bad action' (Upanishad 3.2.13).[33] It is not clear whether this is referring to a ritual performance or an ethical issue; however good action is spoken of later in the *Upanishads* (4.4.7) as action without desire, reinforcing the ethical dimension to *karma*.[34]

We read later in the *Upanishads* the development of *karma* controlling rebirth, spoken of in the 'five fire doctrine'. From this point on, all *karma* doctrine would appear to have a link to *samsara*, the cycle of life and rebirth.[35] *Karma* then became known

---

[27] *Hinduism Glossary for Introduction to Religion,* http://www.uwacadweb.uwyo.edu/religionet/er/Hinduism/HGLOSSRY.HTM, cited 30 Nov 2013

[28] Corduan, p2.

[29] Tommi Lehtonen, 'The Notion of Merit in Indian Religions', *Asian Philosophy* 10/3,2000, p195 & Gombrich, p2.

[30] Corduan, pp2-4.

[31] Corduan, pp4-5.

[32] Gombrich, p3.

[33] Lehtonen, p195.

[34] Richard Gombrich, *Karma,* https://www.soas.ac.uk/ssai/keywords/file24806.pdf, cited 6 Oct 2005, p3.

[35] Gombrich, p4.

as that which drives *samsara*, and determines the consequences for one's actions, controlling the rewards or punishments received. Although *karma* is not sin, some have assumed it to have parallels as bad *karma* results in suffering just as with sin.[36]

The *Bhagavad Gita* refers to the effects and fruit of *karma*.[37] But interestingly, the *Bhagavad Gita* teaches to focus on Krishna rather than one's *karma*. This is due to the inevitable s*amsara* regardless of good or bad deeds.[38] The *Bhagavad Gita* suggests that all will be reborn; good actions will result in rebirth, evil actions will result in rebirth and even doing nothing will still result in rebirth. Good and evil actions would appear to have the same outcome, clearly demonstrating that *karma* is not the equivalent of sin.[39]

Hindus are taught, in the *Bhagavad Gita,* that in order to achieve *moksha* there is no 'one size fits all' but three ways to achieve this.[40] These three ways include: *bhakti marga* – liberation through devotion to and love of a god, *jnana marga* – liberation through knowledge and study and meditation or *karma marga* – liberation through good actions, completing one's duty, one's social obligations and creating good *karma*.[41] These three methods are all embedded in the idea of *karma*, doing good will result in good; a works based-theology.[42]

Karma is often expressed in popular culture and is well known and understood; '*Karma*, as virtually everyone recognizes, is the cosmic law of cause and effect, according to which a person's next life will be shaped by his actions in this life.'[43] Put simply, it is you reap what you sow.[44]

In today's society we often hear people refer to their *karma* to explain events occurring in their life. *Karma* is used in society as

---

[36] Corduan, p2.

[37] Corduan, p5.

[38] Corduan, p5.

[39] Corduan, p7.

[40] BEWR, p438.

[41] BEWR, p438 & Baumann, p593.

[42] Alamu, p245.

[43] Corduan, p2.

[44] Alamu, p250.

either retrospective, to blame the past for current events, or looking to the future with a goal to positively influence.[45] Some would use *karma* as an explanation for the existence of suffering in the world, even to suggest that there is no such thing as unmerited suffering, that all suffering is due to actions.[46]

Karma and Christian Thought

The doctrine of *karma* looks at controlling one's destiny oneself and overlooks the notion of sin especially sin against God.[47] Christianity teaches that all have sinned against God (Ps51:4, Rom 3:23) and that the penalty of this sin is death (Rom 6:23), not *samsara* or ongoing rebirth. This idea of sin is essential in understanding the gospel. This contrasting view, that one's own actions influence one's *karma* and therefore the cycle of life, promotes an individualistic way of thinking, and fails to take into account the influence of others on our lives, which is in stark contrast to Christ's redemptive action for the world that is for every sinful person.[48]

The most significant contrast when comparing *karma* and the gospel of Christ is that salvation is a free gift and can never be earned (Rom 6:23, Eph 2:8-9). No *karma* is sufficient to take the place of death, the consequence for sin. The only way to salvation is through repentance and acceptance of this free gift of God's grace (Rom 10:9-10). Although this grace is appealing, freeing nature from the constant rebirth, it requires an acceptance of sin.[49] Christian salvation teaches one way, through Jesus Christ, with no rebirth or cycle.[50]

Although the idea of *karma* can appear to encompass a sense of justice, it allows no space for concepts like forgiveness and grace and avoids a final judgement.[51] *Karma* would suggest that through

---

[45] Gombrich, p1.

[46] Sreenivasa Rao, *The Doctrine of Karma and Dr A.G.Hogg*,
http://www.biblicalstudies.org.uk/pdf/ift/25-1_030.pdf, cited 20 Dec 2012, pp30-34.

[47] Peavy, p4 &Alamu, p258.

[48] Rao, pp32-33.

[49] Peavy, p5.

[50] Alamu, p245.

[51] Peavy, p3.

work, we will better ourselves in the wheel of life and receive *moksha*. As such the obstacle to salvation is the belief in one's *karma*.[52] This is a distinct contrast to Christianity, where sin is the obstacle to salvation, but salvation is reconciliation with God and an eternal life with Him.[53] The idea of *karma* also limits one's purpose in life; it would suggest the only reason for life is to atone for one's wrong doings, allowing no mention of relationship with a creator God.[54] The key to a Christian existence is a relationship with God, being made in His image, to be loved by Him and to love Him (Gen 1:27, 1 John 4:19).

Witnessing to Hindus

The Hindu belief in *karma* is a big hurdle for Christian witness. Hindus are taught that according to the doctrine of *karma*, only the actions they themselves perform will result in a *karmic* outcome. As such they do not believe another's actions can impact their rebirth.[55] Traditional Hindu schools teach that transfer of merit is impossible; just as one experiences one's own pain and pleasure and cannot transfer it to another, so too one's merit or demerit is non- transferable, confirming that others cannot impact one's *karma*.[56] *Advaita* philosopher Sankara taught that *karma* is not able to be given away to another and each must earn their own salvation.[57] The *Mahabharata* confirms this idea that one cannot enjoy the deeds of another.[58] This poses a challenge when explaining that Jesus' death takes our place (Rom 5:7-9).

This contrasts, however, with the teaching that the transfer of merit is a way to avoid bad *karma*. Vedic literature speaks of merit transferred from the gods to those who perform specific ritual. In addition Brahminic funerals participate in the transfer of merit through rituals which are performed for the dead.[59] Indian

---

[52] Corduan, p2.

[53] Corduan, p2.

[54] Rao, p33.

[55] Lehtonen, p189.

[56] Lehtonen, p192.

[57] Lehtonen, p193.

[58] Lehtonen, p193.

[59] Lehtonen, p194.

philosophy also speaks of group *karma*, transfer of merit between people and their ruler. Some also believe in the transfer of merit and acquiring good or bad *karma* through contact with another. Eating food from a Brahmin is thought to provide good *karma*, whereas food from a thief or prostitute would result in bad.[60]

Hindu people see their *karmic* debt as something which needs to be overcome; they are taught what they sow they will reap. Their understanding is that they are born with a '*karmic* account' and their reincarnation is dependent on this.[61] So speaking of Jesus death for our sin (1 Cor 15:3-4) does not carry much weight. However communicating that Jesus died for our 'karmic debt' is both relevant and helpful.[62]

Contextualising our Christian faith is essential to communicating the Gospel. So while many Hindus have not studied the *Bhagavad Gita* or the *Upanishads*, they understand and are aware of the teachings' concepts through music, theatre and other art forms. As such, to communicate the truth of Christianity we need to contextualise this truth into relevant forms of music and art so it is accessible to those embedded in the Indian culture and lifestyle.[63]

It is also important to note the conflict and sacrifice new faith creates in a Hindu family. Cultural identity and family structure are incredibly significant. When a person turns to Christ it can result in fracturing family ties and social structure. As such Christians need to understand and support with grace and love.[64] In fact, maintaining Indian traditions that are not contradictory to Jesus' teaching and using Indian words are helpful when communicating the gospel. For example the term *Khristbhakta* can be used for someone saved by faith, now called to a life of devotion (that is a Hindu background believer).[65] Using the terms 'forgiven' and 'child of God' rather than 'born again', is advisable as Hindus no longer

---

[60] Lehtonen, p195.

[61] Andy Crouch, 'Christ, My Bodhisattva', *Christianity Today,* 51/5 (2007), p34.

[62] Crouch, pp34, 36.

[63] Shailendra Singh, 'Contextualising the Gospel', in *Walking the Way of the Cross with our Hindu Friends* (ed. Ellen M Alexander & Robin Thomson; Interserve International: Grassroots Mission Publications, 2011), pp66-67.

[64] Singh, pp67-68.

[65] Singh, pp70-71.

want to be 'born again', but rather escape the cycle of rebirth.[66] The language used needs to be helpful without causing any barriers to the gospel.

The most effective witness is action, that is demonstrating the power of love and forgiveness (1 Cor 4:20) and displaying the fruit of the spirit (Gal 5:22-23).[67] Patience is required; some Hindus will happily adopt Jesus as another god among others, but not accept Him as the only way. Prayer and patience is essential.[68] Rarely do Hindus come to faith through doctrinal agreements; a life of love is a far greater testimony and a transforming interaction with the Holy Spirit.[69]

Conclusion

The Hindu faith in all its complexities creates quite a challenge for sharing the gospel.[70] *Karma* is a core belief in Hinduism affecting their understanding of 'salvation' and the need to work to earn a better place. In great contrast to this are the Christian truths teaching that salvation is a free gift and that no-one can be saved through works.

It is essential then, in sharing the gospel with Hindus that Christians pray, are patient and demonstrate love and grace. A cultural mind shift is required for a Hindu to accept the gift of eternal life and this is only possible through the work of the Holy Spirit.

---

[66] Benson, p26.

[67] Singh, p70; Benson, p5.

[68] Benson, p11.

[69] Benson, p6-7.

[70] Wesley Ariarajah, *Hindus and Christians – A Century of Protestant Ecumenical Thought,* Grand Rapids, MI: Eerdmans Publishing Co., 1991, p68.

PATHWAY TO PEACE
Zen Buddhist Meditation and Christian Meditation: A Comparative Study

Kate Lim[1]

Introduction

Meditation is an important spiritual discipline in Buddhism and Christianity. In the West there has been a growing attraction to Zen Buddhist meditation.

In the modern age marked by high stress and materialism, the quest of inner peace is being widely pursued. What is the greatest appeal of Buddhism one may ask? Netland and Yandell suggest in essence, that Buddhism "offers the prospect of deep spirituality without having to bother with God".[2]

However, it is not only the non-Christians who are attracted to Zen Buddhism. There is a growing trend towards embracing Zen meditative practices among certain Christian circles. The term "double belonging", popularized by Paul Knitter, is now a position adopted by many Christians who also practice Zen.[3]

Can our understanding of the fundamentals of Christianity and Buddhism be truly complementary in the practice of meditation? The aim of this essay is to compare Christian and Zen meditation

---

[1] Kate Lim obtained her medical degree from The University of Melbourne and subsequently trained as an Infectious Diseases physician. She is undertaking graduate studies with the Melbourne School of Theology via distance learning whilst residing in Canada with her husband and three children.

[2] H.A. Netland, & K.A. Yandell, *Spirituality without God*, Colorado Springs: Paternoster, 2009, pxii.

[3] Thomas Fox, 'Double belonging: Buddhism and Christian Faith' in *National Catholic Reporter,* http://ncronline.org/news/double-belonging-buddhism-and-christian-faith, cited 4 April 2014.

through exploring the purposes, principles and practices of these two great traditions.

Definitions

"Zen" is now a common expression in everyday conversations and has come to mean for the non-religious, "a state of complete and absolute peace".[4] *Zen* is derived from the Chinese transliteration (*chan; zenna* in Japanese) and from the original Sanskrit, '*dhyana'* which means 'meditation'.[5] Zen however, is more than a spiritual discipline of meditation. Christmas Humphreys describes Zen as the "intuitive insight into real living as distinct from mere existence".[6] The fundamental idea is to "come in touch with the inner workings of our being, and to do this in the most direct way possible without resorting to anything external or superadded".[7]

The word "meditate" as translated in the English Bible originates from the Hebrew words, '*hagah'* or '*siah'* and refer to the practice of meditating on God (Ps 63:6), the law of God (Josh 1:8)[8] or on the works and promises of God (Ps 119).[9] J.I Packer explains,

> Meditation is the activity of calling to mind, and thinking over, and dwelling on and applying to oneself, the various things that one knows about the works and ways and purposes and promises of God. It is an activity of holy thought, consciously performed in the presence of God, under the eye of God, by the help of God, as a means of communion with God.[10]

Herein lies the most important and fundamental difference between the two meditative traditions: the complete exclusion of God in one and utter dependence on God in the other.

---

[4] 'Zen', in Urban Dictionary http://www.urbandictionary.com/define.php?term=zen, cited 3 April 2014.

[5] Christmas Humphreys, *Zen Comes West*, London: Curzon Press, 1977, p25.

[6] Humphreys, p180.

[7] D.T. Suzuki, *Introduction to Zen Buddhism*, New York: Causeway Books, 1974, p44.

[8] Ed.: There is a third word "*suwach*" which is only found in Gen 24:63. Some scholars consider it an earlier form of *siyach* as is found in Ps 119:15.

[9] Stephen Renn (ed), 'Meditation' in *Expository Dictionary of Bible Words*, Peabody, MA.: Hendrikson, 2005, p630.

[10] J.I. Packer, *Knowing God*, Downers Grove, IL: IVP, 1973, p20.

The Purpose of Meditation

The primary objective of Zen meditation is to "acquire a new viewpoint for looking into the essence of things", otherwise known as *satori*.[11] Suzuki highlights the purpose of the discipline as disciplining the mind, making it its own master, through an insight into its proper nature.[12] *Satori*, the beginning of true enlightenment is a direct, unmediated awareness of the ultimate nature of reality.[13] The realization of 'absolute nothingness' is in Zen the realization of one's true self.[14]

The Zen ideal is therefore to "let the mind alight nowhere".[15] The state is also described as Japanese as *mu-nen* (no thought), or *mu-shin* (no mind). The mind does not pick and choose or reflect on itself, but is serenely free-flowing, innocent and direct, not encumbered with thought-forms.[16]

A Chinese Zen master once said "Encountering a Buddha, kill the Buddha...only thus does one attain liberation and detachment from all things, thereby becoming completely unfettered and free".[17]

'Freedom' in the Christian context is radically different. Detachment is not an end in itself but should lead to a freedom that allows the individual to find new and richer attachments to God and to other human beings.[18]

This freedom can only be found in encountering God through the saving work of Christ. The true purpose of Christian meditation, and indeed all of Christian living, is to know God and Jesus Christ whom He has sent (Jn 17). The personal knowledge of a personal

---

[11] Suzuki, p88.

[12] Suzuki, p40.

[13] Netland and Yandell, p61.

[14] Masao *Zen and Western Thought,* Honolulu: University of Hawaii Press, 1985, p197.

[15] Humphreys, p72.

[16] Peter Harvey, *An Introduction to Buddhism,* Cambridge: Cambridge University Press, 1990, p272.

[17] Abe, p187.

[18] Morton Kelsey, *The Other Side of Silence,* London: SPCK, 1977, p98.

God is therefore the supreme focus of our thought and deepest desire of our hearts.[19]

Kelsey regards the basic difference between Christian meditation and that of the eastern religion as whether one sees ultimate reality as a Lover to whom one responds or as a pool of cosmic consciousness in which one seeks to lose identity.[20] The nature of ultimate reality is revealed in Christ and his self-sacrificing love. Jesus sums up the law of God as this: "to love God and to love your neighbour as yourselves" (Matt 22:36-40). Christian meditation is therefore a response to the love of God that should result in richer and more loving relationships with other human beings.

If the goal of Zen meditation is to achieve "no-mind", the goal of Christian meditation is to have the "mind of Christ "(1 Cor 2:16).

The Principles of Meditation

The heart of Zen is encapsulated by the four propositions laid down by its founder, the monk Bodhidharma (8th-6th centuries AD):

> *'A special transmission outside the scriptures;*
> *no dependence upon words;*
> *direct pointing to the mind of men;*
> *seeing into one's own nature and the attainment of*
> *Buddhahood'.*[21]

Self-reliance is a fundamental principle of Buddhism. Zen takes this a step further and emphasizes on 'self-realisation', rejecting the authority of anything external, be it God or any scriptures. In this sense, it stands outside traditional Buddhism for it is not based on any Buddhist scripture but claims it returns directly to the root and source of all forms of Buddhism.[22]

The emphasis is on the search within and absolute faith is placed in man's own inner being.[23] Zen's main thesis is to see into the work

---

[19] Campbell McAlpine, *The Practice of Christian Meditation*, London: Marshall Pickering, 1981, p9.

[20] Kelsey, p1.

[21] Humphreys, p23.

[22] Abe, p194.

[23] Suzuki, p44.

of creation independent from a creator. Suzuki claims "Zen wants absolute freedom, even from God".[24]

Contrast this with Christian meditation, which is entirely centered on God. The heart of Christian meditation is God himself. Clowney highlights three distinctives of Christian meditation: "it is centered on the truth of God, moved by the love of God, directed to the praise of God".[25]

Not only is God indispensable in Christian meditation; the practice of meditation is fully dependent on inspiration of the Holy Spirit and Holy Scriptures. The truth of God is revealed by the Holy Spirit, through the scriptures (Jn 16:13). The true revelation of God is what we seek when we meditate on God and his written word. The self is fully surrendered to God, "crucified with Christ", that we may experience God living in us (Gal 2:20). Slade further expounds:

> Becoming identified with Christ in the center of our being is much more than becoming like him and sharing his perfect human nature. It is a participation in divine nature. By sharing the perfection of the Lord's humanity we become capable of sharing his divinity, without being annihilated. It is as sons that we find our loving union with our Father. This is an essential principle of Christian meditation.[26]

The Practice of Meditation

The techniques of Zen meditation focus on developing high states of awareness. It aims at first calming the mind and then sustained concentration. It is through this activity that the true nature of oneself and its universe will reveal itself.

Zazen is a form of sitting meditation emphasizing a correct posture conducive for the mind. To assist in controlling wandering thoughts, the meditator is encouraged to count and follow the breath. Expressed simply the practice of *Zazen* is to just sit and maintain awareness of your experience without getting caught up in assessing, comparing, or trying to change it. The meditator sets

---

[24] Suzuki, p97.

[25] Edmund Clowney, *Christian Meditation,* New Jersey: Craig Press, 1979, p91.

[26] Herbert Slade, *Meeting Schools of Oriental Meditation,* London: Lutterworth, 1973, p32.

out to just sit with no deliberate thought. If thoughts nevertheless arise, he just lets them pass by without comment. The practice should lead to an effortless watching, and the development of a strong one-pointed concentration. This is otherwise known as the state of "self-mastery *Samadhi*" (*jishuzammai* in Japanese), which means to "access" concentration.[27]

Zazen prepares the mind for mastering the *koan*, the aim of which is to open one's mind to the truth of Zen. *Koan* is often an anecdote of an ancient master, or a dialogue between a master and monks, or a statement or question put forward by a teacher. In *koan* mediation, the meditator contemplates the critical word or point in an enigmatic *koan* story or statement in an attempt to shut up all possible avenues to rationalization and push the mind to its furthest limit.[28]

When one masters a *koan*, "the conceptual reasoning mind has reached its absolute dead-end, and the bottom of the mind is broken through, so that the flow of thoughts suddenly stops, in a state of no-thought, and realization erupts from the depths".[29] This is when *satori* is realized, when one possesses a "direct intuitive looking into the nature of things in contradiction to the analytical or logical understanding of it".[30]

What does a high state of awareness mean for a Christian? Calhoun provides a helpful description of Christian contemplative prayer as "waking up to the presence of God in all things".[31] Indeed, when Christians engage in meditation and contemplation, it is about sitting in the presence of God. It is a restful waiting on the Lord, allowing the Holy Spirit to bring our heart and minds into focus on himself and his word. In the stillness of our hearts and mind, we encounter the living God (Ps. 46:10).

The focus on breath as a meditative technique has long been used in Christian traditions as well. Breath prayer is a form of contemplative prayer linked to the rhythms of breathing and the

---

[27] Harvey, p271.
[28] Suzuki, p108.
[29] Harvey, p273.
[30] Suzuki, p230.
[31] Calhoun, p48.

Eastern orthodox church sees breath prayer has a way of living out Paul's instruction to "pray without ceasing" (1 Thess 5:17).[32]

The idea of "breath" for the Christian is a reminder of our creator God who breathed life into man and who created us to worship him. The psalmist declares "let everything that has breath praise the Lord" (Ps 150:6). Indeed, true meditation brings a response to God, be it in the form of self-examination and confession of sin, or a heartfelt worship of his greatness and goodness.

The psalmist meditated on the laws and precepts of God, on the works of God and on his promises (Ps 119). In practical terms today, meditation is a devotional practice of pondering the words of a verse, or verses of scripture, with a receptive heart, allowing the Holy Spirit to take the written word and apply it as the living word to the inner being.[33] The result is imparting divine truth that is only possible through revelation by the Holy Spirit (1 Cor 2:9-13). We believe the scriptures to be living and active (Heb 4:12). Meditation on scriptures trains us to be mentally alert and spiritually watchful.

Double Belonging: Can Buddhism and Christianity be complementary?

Knitter reflects on "double belonging" as being "genuinely nourished by more than one religious tradition".[34] This is a spiritually enticing prospect for the sincere seeker wishing to experience spirituality without being bound by traditional religious dogmas and legalism.

Zen is openly inclusive and invites people from all faiths to participate in its practice. Christians who have embraced Zen have found that Buddhism provides Christians with the techniques by which they can enter more experientially into the content of what they believe.

---

[32] Calhoun, p205.

[33] MacAlpine, p75.

[34] Fox, *Double belonging.*

Proponents of double belonging emphasize that Zen is non-theistic as opposed to atheistic and hence not contradictory to the Christian faith. The idea of double belonging is not new and was already propagated in the last century by Thomas Merton. Merton saw Zen as "consciousness unstructured by particular form or systems, a trans-cultural, trans-religious, trans-formed consciousness".[35]

Buddhism is non-theistic in the sense that it neither affirms nor denies the existence of God. Its principal thesis however, is that God is not necessary. Zen is not so much a non-theistic 'consciousness' but a 'consciousness' that does not want anything to do with God.

Much of Merton's encounter with Zen was through dialogue with D.T. Suzuki, widely regarded in the West as the most influential Zen master. Suzuki himself however writes blatantly that Christianity is "too conscious of God". Quoting Acts 17:28 *'in him we live and move and have our being'*, he says "Zen wants to have this last trace of God consciousness, if possible, obliterated".[36]

Here is the crux of the matter: Zen outrightly rejects God. As Humphrey puts it, "Zen practice has no use for God".[37]

While it is important in interfaith dialogues to establish similarities between the faiths, in order to have an honest conversation, we would need to admit that the similarities are superficial and the differences deep.

Suzuki is on the offensive when he scoffs at the contemplations and prayers of St Ignatius as, from Zen point of view, "merely so many fabrications of the imagination elaborately woven for the benefit of the piously minded; and in reality this is like piling tiles upon tiles on one's head, and there is no true gain in the life of the spirit". He is right in saying "there is not a shadow of similitude between the exercises of Zen and those proposed by the founder of the Society of Jesus".[38]

---

[35] Thomas Merton, *Zen and the Birds of Appetite*, New York: New Directions, 1968, p4.

[36] Suzuki, p132.

[37] Humphrey, p72.

[38] Suzuki, p42.

What we are faced with are two radically different perspectives on reality, on the nature of man and the need for a saviour. The two cannot be complementary but contradictory.

Conclusion

A comparative study on Zen and Christian meditation is fraught with difficulties for they cannot be seen simply as two alternative pathways to inner peace. Zen says it is "the act of walking on, but there is no path, no walker and no goal",[39] while Christianity insists Jesus is the only way, the truth and the life; the Prince of Peace who promises peace that surpasses understanding.

Not only do the same terminologies often mean something entirely different in the two meditative traditions, but also the fundamental difference is clear: that of the necessity of God and centrality of Christ's saving work. These are fundamental to Christian meditation but removed and rejected by Zen.

Perhaps the most important lesson we need to learn from our friends who practice Zen is the priority of disciplining our mind through meditation. Packer reminds us that "Christians suffer grievously from their ignorance of the practice" of meditation.[40] Indeed, it is only when meditation becomes an integral part of our Christian life, do we truly experience what it means to live a blessed life.

Blessed is the one...
... whose delight is in the law of the Lord,
and who meditates on his law day and night....
That person is like a tree
planted by streams of water,
which yields its fruit in season
and whose leaf does not wither
whatever they do prospers.
Psalm 1:1-3

---

[39] Humphrey, p27.
[40] Packer, p20.

ISLAM, THE CROSS, AND CHRIST VICTORIOUS

Brent Neely[1]

A Crucial Divide

The crucifixion of Christ is a classic point of contention between Christianity and Islam. For Christians, the cross is the core symbol of our faith, a cosmic event, and the fulcrum on which human salvation turns.[2] On the other hand, the traditional Islamic rejection of the death of Christ (and the entailed atonement theology) is unequivocal, and frequently vehement. Todd Lawson calls the crucifixion of Jesus "probably the greatest single obstacle" in the Christian-Muslim relationship.[3] The cross of Christ remains a "stumbling block" in the Muslim world.

In this paper we will examine a few common Islamic objections to the Christian doctrine of the atonement through the crucifixion of Jesus, particularly theological or ideological[4]; complaints that a theology of redemption by the cross is irrational or altogether unworthy of Almighty God. We are especially concerned with the charge that cross-theology speaks of a "weak" God. In response we advocate in part for a more robust presentation of the *Christus Victor* paradigm of the atonement.

Traditional Muslim textual authorities have over time produced very theologically pointed interpretations of Q 4:157ff., the only

---

[1]Brent Neely has served in the Middle East with the Arabic-speaking church and in theological education for the past eighteen years; during much of that period he has been active on the executive committee of the Evangelical Alliance Israel. He would like to thank Eloise Neely for input on the style and presentation of the material in this essay.

[2] Christian speech about the cross is in many respects a sort of theological shorthand for the *whole soteriological complex of the death-burial-resurrection-ascension-reign of Christ.* This paper is primarily concerned with the issue of the actual crucifixion and death of Jesus.

[3] Todd Lawson, *The Crucifixion and the Qur'an, A Study in the History of Muslim Thought,* Oxford: Oneworld, 2009, p95.

[4] As opposed to "historically" or "socially" grounded claims such as attacks on the veracity of the gospels or those related to the issue of the Crusades.

171

qur'anic text mentioning the (non) crucifixion of Christ. Classical Sunni exegesis has particularly used hadiths (prophetic traditions) to fill in the pronounced semantic and narrative gaps in Q 4:157f, an ambiguous, allusive, and linguistically disputable text. This has eventuated in the standard Islamic position that the crucifixion never happened to Jesus, but that somehow God intervened, rescued him, and raised him to heaven from whence he will one day return to establish Islam throughout the earth. Typically this view entails God engineering a "substitute" who is killed instead of Jesus. On sophisticated literary-philological, historical-critical, and theological grounds, some modern scholars have strongly argued that this traditional understanding of the text misconstrues the rhetorical intent of the Qur'an. On this reading the text really only denies the success of "the Jews" in confounding God's purposes; *it may not, in fact, deny that Jesus died on the cross*.[5] However that may be, such literary-critical argumentation holds virtually no water for most Muslims.[6] For the Muslim, the ultimate arbiter of truth is the Qur'an, or rather, *the Qur'an as it has been authoritatively understood in Islamic tradition*.[7] On these grounds, the crucifixion of Jesus is categorically and unambiguously denied.

The substitution theory,[8] and most especially the denial of the crucifixion of Jesus, dominates the all-important classical Sunni commentary tradition, and remains virtually required orthodoxy in mainstream Islam to our day. In his Qur'an commentary, the Islamist ideologue, Sayyid Qutb (d. 1966), holds that the historical record on the crucifixion is thoroughly obfuscated and thus the truth can only be known via (qur'anic) revelation. For him, we cannot know the mode of Jesus' gathering to heaven (body and soul, or soul only?), but we must hold (with the Qur'an) that he was neither killed nor crucified by the Jews; it seems another victim

---

[5] Cf. Gabriel Said Reynolds, "The Muslim Jesus: Dead or Alive?" *BSOAS* 72.2, 2009, p237-258.

[6] There are more modernist or "progressive" Muslim intellectuals who do allow for the death of Jesus on the cross (as, historically, have certain Sufis and particular Shi'is). Cf. Mahmoud Ayoub, "Towards an Islamic Christology, II, The Death of Jesus, Reality or Delusion," *Muslim World* 70.2, 1980. This does not result in Jesus as atoning saviour.

[7] As Lawson points out, it is not so much the Qur'an, but mainstream *Muslim commentary* (*tafsir*) *on it*, which denies the crucifixion of Jesus (Lawson, *The Crucifixion*, p95). Standard Sunni commentary is dominated by the Substitution view; there is a surprising, but marginal, stream of dissident opinion on this point in the history of *tafsir*.

[8] Originating in many Muslim hadiths, and not to be confused with the Christian teaching of the "substitutionary atonement."

was provided.[9] The famous Egyptian commentary from the early twentieth century, the *Manar Commentary* (*Tafsir al-Manar*), in the section by the Islamic reformer Rashid Rida (d. 1935) on Q 4:157, includes a lengthy, highly polemical[10] attack on the atonement of the cross from historical, textual, philosophical, and theological angles.[11] (In an appendix we provide a translation of one segment of this treatise.)

As Kenneth Cragg puts it, "Islamic convictions about Jesus and the Cross have never simply been those of mere investigators dealing with evidence. They have been those of believers persuaded already by theology."[12] In the *Manar Commentary*, Rashid Rida, puts the contrast between Muslim and Christian views of salvation, the cross, and much else, sharply and starkly:

> The truth is that Islam is the religion of Muhammad and the Messiah and all the prophets. But it is not possible to combine the religion of the Qur'an (which is without error and cannot be contradicted) and the paulinist religion, which is based on the premise that three-are-one and one-is three and also on the pagan-redemption-doctrine of the crucifixion. How can one combine *tawhid* (Islamic monotheism) and Trinity? Or how can one combine the doctrine of salvation by one's faith in a Lord who curses himself and tortured himself for the sake of his own servants, even though [God's] purposes [of salvation] still might not be achieved through all this?[13]

The rhetorical stance of the Qur'an is frequently polemical, very often set against a sectarian opponent (Jewish, Christian, or pagan).[14] This is also true of some of the Sunni apocalyptic hadiths

---

[9] Sayyid Qutb, *In the Shade of the Qur'an* v. 3, p316-318 [an English translation, apparently by the Islamic Foundation (Leicester, UK), available online at: http://www.kalamullah.com/shade-of-the-quran.html, accessed 19 May 2015.

[10] For example, attacking the historical value of the New Testament gospels while leaning on the dubious Gospel of Barnabas. On the Gospel of Barnabas, see A.H. Mathias Zahniser, *The Mission and Death of Jesus in Islam and Christianity*, Marynoll, NY: Orbis, 2008, chap. 6.

[11] See Zahniser, *Mission and Death*, p59-60.

[12] Kenneth Cragg, *Jesus and the Muslim, An Exploration*, Oxford: Oneworld, 2003, p178.

[13] *Tafsir al-Manar* on Q 4:157 available here (in Arabic): http://www.altafsir.com/Tafsir.asp?tMadhNo=0&tTafsirNo=103&tSoraNo=4&tAyahNo=157&tDisplay=yes&Page=36&Size=1&LanguageId=1 accessed 27 June 2015.

[14] Cf. Sidney Griffith, *The Bible in Arabic: The Scriptures of the "People of the Book" in the Language of Islam*, Princeton: Princeton University Press, 2013, Kindle Edition, locations 330-765, and G.S. Reynolds, "On the Presentation of Christianity in the Qur'an and the Many Aspects of Qur'anic Rhetoric," *Al-Bayan* 12, 2014, p42-54.

which esteemed Muslim commentators have integrated with the interpretation of Q 4:157ff., expanding the circle of ire beyond the so-called "People of the Book" to also include Shi'i "heretics."[15] Taken as a whole, the agendas accompanying the story of the Muslim Jesus escaping the cross and returning at the End, cover issues of polemics, soteriology, prophetology, and eschatology. There are myriad potential Muslim objections to a theology of the cross; in this essay we examine only a narrow sampling.

Here (below) we present a few short excerpts from Rida's lengthy reflections on and fulminations against Christian atonement theory by way of exegesis of Q 4:157ff.[16] Rida's rhetoric is highly caricatured and tendentious, displaying a marked tone-deafness to the Christian narrative structure of salvation and its trinitarian dynamic. Neither is there any acknowledgment of the irreducible tensions common to *all* monotheistic conviction.[17] As may be seen throughout Rida's expostulation against atonement theology,[18] any given instance of protest against "cross theology" may actually integrate multiple and overlapping concerns. The heaviest emphasis throughout the larger diatribe is clearly on the "absurdity," "immorality," or "illogicality" of the Christian redemption story. But alongside all this flows a related undercurrent—an angry sense that the story bespeaks a sort of pathos or weakness on the part of God.

For example:

> As if, when [God] created Adam, he did not know what would happen with him; and when Adam transgressed [God] did not know what justice and mercy required in that case, until [God] finally came upon the solution after thousands of years had passed in the created order. It implies ... [God's] being caught in the problem of the contradiction between [justice and mercy].

---

[15] Cf. Reynolds and "Muslim Jesus," p249-251.

[16] In the appendix we provide a translation of more of this segment of Rida's writing. These excerpts and their larger context may be found at: *Tafsir al-Manar* (http://www.altafsir.com/Tafasir.asp?tMadhNo=0&tTafsirNo=103&tSoraNo=4&tAyahNo= 157&tDisplay=yes&Page=12&Size=1&LanguageId=1 [advancing from this web page to the following one, using the internal paging function], accessed 15 July 2015—Arabic text.

[17] See below on "mystery" and transcendence.

[18] See appendix.

...Whoever accepts this [salvation] story is required to surrender to what every independent mind would reject as impossible, that the creator of the universe should become incarnate in the womb of a woman on this earth which is accounted as less than an atom by comparison with the rest of his realm and with the heavens you see from this earth. And then to become human, to eat, drink, tire, and undergo whatever else humans experience. And then his enemies take him by force and abuse and crucify him with the thieves, and make him cursed according to the ruling of a scripture which he gave to some of his messengers. God Most High be exalted above all that!

...This [salvation] story requires something even worse than attributing to the Creator the inability to accomplish his will in bringing together justice and mercy; that is, [the story requires] the total eradication of justice and mercy in the crucifixion of the Messiah, since God punished him as a human not deserving punishment, for he was in no way guilty.

The Cross: Illogical and Weak?

To approximate Cragg's turn of phrase, the mainline Islamic position with respect to whether the crucifixion of Jesus happened is that historically it did not, redemptively it need not, and morally it should not.[19]   Rashid Rida powerfully exemplifies these misgivings. Our purpose here is to selectively examine some of these theological challenges, not to respond to Rida in detail. Nonetheless, he will be a useful point of reference.

One way of viewing the cluster of criticisms that interest us is to present the complaints in a binary fashion: (a) the cross is "illogical" and (b) it is "shameful." Under the rubric of "illogical" (a), may be filed charges against the cross' "practical" *and* "moral" rationality. That is, it "makes no sense" for God to save or judge with respect to the cross, for God is well able to forgive, or not, simply by sovereign fiat. Beyond that, in terms of substitutionary atonement, it is morally ineffective, if not repugnant, for one to bear the guilt of an unworthy other. The cross is found to be "ethically non-sensical."

---

[19] *Jesus and the Muslim*, p178.

As to the other category of objection, the cross is "shameful" (b), we face the problem of the dishonor the passion of Christ would seem to impute not only to a revered prophet (Jesus), but also to God himself. Concomitant with this would be the argument that the whole enterprise of the crucifixion would be a massive show of weakness, ultimately, weakness attributed to Almighty God! Because of limitations of space, we shall do little more than briefly touch on the important complaint about the "illogicality" of the cross. Primarily we turn our attention to the claim that the cross of Christ is a shameful doctrine, and especially to the idea that it inexcusably presents a God who is weak and constrained.

Theology, Ontology, and Anthropology

Some of the difficulty of communicating about the crucifixion across the religious divide lies with theological or philosophical commitments that are so basic that we often fail to examine them ourselves. In this discussion, we are not always grappling with conscious theology but rather with the realm of foundational (and incompatible) worldviews. A part of the struggle around the validity, or not, of the atonement stems from a gaping divide in the assumptions about the nature of God, humanity, and even "reality."

With respect to the nature of God, one can, for example, sense a tangible frustration running through the comments we translated from the *Manar*. Rida veritably bellows that *God does not need* such elaborate and costly schemes (as the cross) to effect salvation. Allah is great, powerful, and far above all that! For Rida, the costly, painful, historical development of salvation-history, climaxing in the cross, puts unacceptable limits on the unbounded, unchallenged, unconstrained Allah. He can simply judge or forgive as he sees fit (presumably in line with "justice"). But, we face here an irreducible conflict of worldviews. In this exchange, the Muslim and Christian are differing over the nature of God, yes, but not only so—we differ over the nature of God *and* (his) reality itself.

At the danger of oversimplification, for the Muslim there is no more necessary assertion than the "greatness" of God; his power, volition, and capacities must be untrammeled in every way. To posit that the demands of justice and mercy "required" the sacrifice of the cross is "infuriating presumption." Conversely, for the

Christian, there is no doubting the greatness or omnipotence of God, nor do we place outside constraints on the King. Rather, for us, the cross as the meeting point of justice and mercy is simply a reflection of the nature of the cosmos, of the moral universe. No one is "placing" any boundaries on God, but rather we seek (in the light of revelation) to describe *his* universe as it in fact is. The cross highlights an irreconcilable divergence in Christian and Muslim ontologies.

Tied in to all of this is a similar divide on the question of spiritual anthropology.[20]   On this count too, beyond questions of divine justice or mercy (both posited of God in the Qur'an), and beyond questions of divine power (the Qur'an's God is able to judge, forgive, and "guide" wayward humanity with effortless decree), we have a yawning chasm of ontology—the question of what the human condition and human need actually is. What is required for wholeness, for rectifying the relationship between humanity and God?   In Islam "problem and solution" come off as relatively simple.[21]   As Rida puts it, Islam is the faith of "knowledge and effort." All that is required is divine guidance and human action to correct human "straying."   At best, then, the cross becomes superfluous.

On a New Testament view, a crucifixion in ancient Palestine reveals our common condition: the darkness, degradation, and destruction of this event highlight the depth of human hurt, loss, and need. The cross represents a starkly realistic evaluation of our spiritual state, a metric of human evil. Salvation to be effective must intersect at the juncture of our tragedy. On the cross it does. An over-optimistic assessment of the human condition, the glossing over or minimizing of our moral brokenness, is as spiritually and socially dangerous as is a morose pessimism and despair. But, painful and dark as it must appear at first blush, a theology of the cross speaks power and hope to humanity in its darkened state. In the cross, as both fact and symbol, the tragedy of human sin is taken at its fullest measure, and evil, being borne by Christ, is borne away.[22]

---

[20] Cf. Duane Alexander Miller, "Narrative and Metanarrative in Christianity and Islam," *St. Francis Magazine* 6.3, 2010, p501-516.

[21] Conceptually speaking. No claim is made that moral exertion (*ijtihad*) is easy or lacking in the Muslim community.

[22] Closely paraphrasing Cragg, *Jesus and the Muslim*, p179.

The Cross and Mystery

Beyond the elusive questions of ontology, people of faith cannot expound the cross, salvation, or even existential questions generally, while excluding transcendence and mystery. With respect to the present topic, there is indeed some mystery in terms of "how" a cosmic transaction is effected in the atonement of the cross. The "internal mechanics" of redemption may forever remain beyond our comprehension, but revelation and experience indicate something of both the "how" and of the "why" of our salvation. At the heart of the former is, marvellously, the cross. Built-in to the latter are considerations of God's glory and the infinite love of the Father. For all its incredulity with respect to atonement theory, Islam itself is hardly a stranger to problems at the boundaries of human epistemology, the interface between the transcendent Eternal and the finite mortal.[23]

One locus of mystery is what the cross tells us of the nature of God. Biblical reflection on the cross is intimately linked to *God incarnate* and *God as Trinity*. Beginning with one "sticking point" (the cross), we end up alighting on another. Note Rida's incomprehension of and disdain for the "paulinist" Trinity. In the atonement we have one God, but distinct "persons" acting in concert for human rescue.[24] The cross is an intricate action of divine revelation, revealing not only the Son, but also Father and Spirit, the *self-giving God* acting *for* us.[25]

Yes, the convergence of love and power, mercy and justice at the cross is a divine "foolishness" which trumps human wisdom (1 Cor. 1:25; Cf. 1 Cor. 1:17-18, 24, 30). The cross is the last-days intervention, a mystery now "revealed" (Rom. 1:17; Greek:

---

[23] I think here of problems such as creation and time, divine sovereignty and human free will, divine action in history, and the eternality of the (Arabic!) Qur'an as a category integral to, but distinct from, God himself.

[24] The gift of life through the death on a cross is not an *external* action performed to propitiate a barely willing Judge; it is not a Father brutalizing an innocent Son for the crimes of a third party.

[25] Cf. Jn 10:17-18; Acts 20:28; Rom. 3:5, 21-26; 5:8-11; 2 Cor. 5:19; Gal. 2:20; Eph. 5:2; 1 Pet. 2:24; Rev. 5:9. The logic of Isaiah's Suffering Servant is relevant here: the action of one servant for the many, is simultaneously the action of God for his people.

apokalyptetai). The wonder of the death and resurrection of the Messiah was an unanticipated drama on behalf of human salvation, a mystery which confounds... until scales fall from eyes (cf. 1 Cor. 2:6-8; 2 Cor. 3:12-4.6; Eph. 2:1-9; 4.17-24).

A Question of Justice

As stated, we do not have the space to thoroughly consider the objection that the cross is unacceptable on logical and/or moral grounds, or, simply, that such a redemption would be "unjust."[26] As we discern in Rida's comments, he finds the Islamic exhortation to human will, choice, and self-purification (with repentance) a far superior path to salvation than the "pathetic ignorance" of the "Christian cross".[27] The acclaimed scholar Fazlur Rahman squarely dismissed the notion of a redeemer, savior, or intercessor.[28] Clearly, the concept of a vicarious redemption is a raw nerve when it comes to Christian and Islamic ideas of salvation.[29] Unfortunately, Christians themselves have at times promulgated crass versions of a substitutionary atonement in which the guilty escapes scot-free while the innocent is arbitrarily punished, a sort of "shuffling of the cards."[30]

However, on a New Testament reckoning, we must insist, at the Cross, justice is by no means ignored. "Substitutionary sacrifice" is hardly the exclusive paradigm through which to view the cross (see below), but even within this paradigm, sin is not casually "transferred to another's account." In fact, without cosmic and costly intervention, sin cannot simply be obviated, even on grounds of repentance, good works, "mere" mercy, or judicial ruling. Rather,

---

[26] Cragg's work, cited in this essay, actively tackles this challenge.

[27] Cf. Yusuf H.R. Seferta, "The Ideas of Muhammad 'Abduh and Rashid Ridha Concerning Jesus," *Encounter* 124 (Pontificio Istituto di Studi Arabi e d'Islamistica), 1986, p10-11.

[28] Interestingly, though, he did acknowledge the strong "psychological factor involved in the ideas of intercession and redemption," even for Muslims; *Major Themes of the Qur'an*, Mineapolis: Bibliotheca Islamica, 1980, p31.

[29] Set in its most appealing light, the Qur'an is emphatic about both the justice and mercy of God. It is a standard truism that each one must bear their own guilt, no one bearing the sin of another (e.g., Q 2:286; 6:164; 35:18; 39:7; cf. Ps. 49:7).

[30] *Jesus and the Muslim*, p181. Cf. Cragg, "The Qur'an and the Cross," p182. In a different context, Nijay Gupta refers to a simplistic style of "justification theory" as little more than "heavenly paperwork" that expunges sin (see https://academic.logos.com/2014/02/04/new-testament-scholarship-50-books-everyone-should-read-part-2-paul/, accessed 23 May 2015.

consequent on the cross, sin is decisively answered, *in part* by the categories of the believer's identification and participation with Christ and their transformation and regeneration. Somehow, in union with Christ, what happened to Messiah, has happened to us.[31] Sin is reckoned with, not brushed under the carpet.

The "Shame" of the Crucifixion:
Does the Cross Demean God?

There is considerable angst and antagonism on the part of most Muslims to the notion that God would allow his great prophet, Jesus, to bear the ignominy of crucifixion.[32] But it gets worse: by logical extension, in sanctioning the cross, the very honor and greatness of God himself would also seem to be in question. God comes off looking rather weak.[33] Does not the cross proclaimed by the apostles demean God himself? That is not God's way, for, after all, "God is great" (*allahu akbar*)! In any case, God has no need to stoop to such unworthy measures to save and to forgive. The whole superstructure of atonement theory is (for Islam) an undignified and unnecessary construct. Forgiveness is easy for God: As easy as was his creation of Adam himself; he need only say "Be... and it is" (Q 3:59)."[34]

But, it is at this very point that Christian thought inverts Islamic intuition: In seeking to aggrandize God, Muslims may be limiting him, even if by time-honoured dogma. We should not disallow his "stooping" in compassion and unearned condescension to his creatures.[35] Yes, it may well be that such humility on the part of the King offends us. Indeed, the sting of offense is there in the earliest record of the apostolic preaching (1 Cor. 1:2-23). The cross portrays the depths to which God descended in order to lift us. The cross hurts. It hurts our pride, our self-view, our presumed status

---

[31] Cf. Ida Glaser, "Cross-Reference Theology: Speaking, Thinking, and Living the Cross in the Context of Islam," in *Jesus and the Cross*," p148. Cf. Rom. 6:4, 8:17, 13:14; Phil. 3:10-11; Col. 3:1-4; 2 Tim 2:11-12.

[32] Atonement theory also presents an inverse problem: Jesus as either Suffering Servant or Anointed Son and Saviour violates the essential soteriology and prophetology of the Qur'an and casts an unacceptably deep shadow over Muhammad himself.

[33] Note again Rida's astonishment that God should have to jump through all these implausible and dishonourable hoops to achieve salvation.

[34] *Jesus and the Muslim*, p180.

[35] *Jesus and the Muslim*, p180-181.

and self-sufficiency. The truth is, we must be hurt to be healed (Hos. 6:1-3).

The cross was from the start a token of shame, a political and social horror in the ancient world. Christ and his cross remain a stone of stumbling in our world today. But at a deep level, the real cause of the offense lies not in any supposed "weakness" attributed to God; no, the offense lies in the fact that the cross exposes *our* shame. Bill Musk points out that, even as the Passion may for some imply a "loss of honor," the whole narrative is pregnant with a mysterious sense of Jesus' power: through his brave and *honorable* fidelity to God—even to death on a cross—he transforms the shame achieving life, victory, and glory.[36] The effect is hardly to demean God; the cross resounds with his glory.

Christus Victor and the Power of the Cross

In the passages from Rida (above) there is palpable scorn towards the "weakness" of the Christian redemption story: he ridicules the thought that God should not immediately "know" what to do; that any "inability" should be attributed to him; that he should accept the smallness and humiliation of entering the world (let alone a womb) and submitting to abuse and the curse of the cross. It is all revoltingly "weak!"

Too often Muslim approaches to our Gospel have misconstrued the story as one of defeatism and a morbid obsession with weakness, death, and loss—a tale of effete pacifism. However, whatever else may be said about this criticism, it certainly fails to even attempt an understanding "from within." Without equivocation, Christians glory in the cross, an ostensible symbol of loss, death, and shame. But *why?* Because it is also the miraculous site of God's cosmic victory, brilliantly executed to his glory and for our salvation—a salvation precisely *from* those things (loss, death, shame) in which humanity is enmeshed by sin. Death is undone by death (Heb. 2:14). It *is* a paradoxical story, but a story of power and glory nonetheless.

---

[36] Bill Musk, *Touching the Soul of Islam*, Crowborough, UK: MARC, 1995, p83. Cf. Zahniser, *Mission and Death*, p238f; Cragg, *Jesus and the Muslim*, p167-168 (the sufferer's "will for" the cross); *idem,* "The Qur'an and the Cross," p182-183.

In the New Testament there are multiple modes or images of the atonement achieved on the cross of Christ.[37] Michael Bird suggests that the one mode best suited to integrate and correlate all the others is that of *the cross (and resurrection) as the manifest victory of Jesus over the evil powers—sin, hell, and death*—that is, the *Christus Victor* model.

The Christus Victor model places Jesus' death in its proper coordinates as an apocalyptic event that reveals God's rescue plan against the evil powers (see Gal 1: 4). Evidently Jesus' substitutionary death constitutes the basis and center of the divine victory— a victory not only against sin but also against Satan... Thus Jesus' substitutionary death for sinners is the means to the cosmic triumph of God's purposes for God's people leading to God's new creation. This seems to mesh with the theological contours of Romans 8 and 1 Corinthians 15 that move from atonement to triumph... Jesus' death for sinners on the cross is part of a bigger picture that is laid out in redemptive history, visible in the very shape of our canon, apparent in biblical theology, ubiquitous in historical theology, and explicit in Pauline theology. The doctrines of penal substitution and Christus Victor do not compete against each other, for the former is clearly the grounds for the latter.[38]

Sacrificial, substitutionary, or "levitical" imagery is native to the early Christian exposition of the cross (cf. Rom. 3:23-26, 5:9-11; Eph. 5:2; 1 Jn 4:10). However, when set against Jewish expectation in the first century, the role of a Messiah was not *primarily* that of offering himself as a "blood sacrifice" for the sins of the people, let alone the world. No, if a dominant messianic image might be discerned at all, surely it would be one of a warrior King, rescuing Israel from pagan power and oppression, delivering victory, and leading her to national renewal, covenant blessing, and a glorious age of divine favour.

---

[37] Michael Bird notes eight such modes; *Evangelical Theology: A Biblical and Systematic Introduction*, Grand Rapids: Zondervan, 2013, section 4.4.1.

[38] *Evangelical Theology*, Kindle Locations 9278-9286 and 9295-9297. Further on penal substitution see:
http://www.patheos.com/blogs/euangelion/2015/06/atonement-as-payment-or-forgiveness/, accessed 14 June 2015.

The Messiah of the New Testament surprisingly is presented as both fulfilling and subverting this messianic expectation.[39] Jesus does indeed come in power as king ("declared with power to be the Son of God") and leads the people of God out of bondage into the "glorious freedom of the sons of God," unseating all illegitimate authority and the sway of evil. He fulfils the paschal expectation of a second great Exodus, upending false deities and liberating slaves, now sons and daughters receiving their inheritance. The Lord indeed ushers in God's rule, but, the story pivots on an unanticipated axis—the cross. Shockwaves emanate from the crucifixion which reveals that the enemy unseated is not "pagan Rome," but sin and the oppressive powers that exploit the fallen human heart, not least the hearts of the "chosen people" themselves; and the objects of God's redemption are, counter-intuitively, both the Jews and "the nations."[40]

However likely or not, and however contrary to conventional expectation, the story of the cross is indeed a story of <u>power</u>, a story of the conquering king. Every layer and genre of the New Testament is replete with this theme of Christus Victor, the Messiah resplendent. In the crucifixion, vindicated by resurrection, the world is remade, humanity reborn, Jews and Gentiles reconciled, Jesus exalted to the highest station, and principalities and powers thrown down (Acts 2:32-36; Eph. 1:7, 19-23; 2:13-17). The cross is the locus of a pitched battle were humans are set free from sin and the blight of evil is publicly undone (Col. 2:13-15). The Passion is a subversive story of victory—of life through death, of gain through loss, of triumph in suffering.

In the synoptic tradition and Acts, Jesus' ministry is portrayed as one of forgiveness but also as a work of liberation, of overthrowing the devil, and of *power* (cf. Acts 10:38; 26:18). Jesus, the rejected King of the passion stories, is committed, faithful, and resolute under pressure, temptation, and violent opposition—relentless in his mission, even when deserted by his own. "He set his face towards Jerusalem." There is no question of the strength of this

---

[39] Compare Darrell L. Bock, "Embracing Jesus in a First Century Context: What Can It Teach Us About Spiritual Commitment?" *Journal of Spiritual Formation & Soul Care*, 3.2, 2010; sections on Jewish and Greco-Roman context.

[40] Note, then, that in this assessment of the accomplishment of the crucified Lord, forgiveness of sin retains its vital place, even when the cross is viewed as a sort of "military victory."

Jesus *to, before*, and *on* the cross.[41] Further, in terms of power, in the Passion story there are plenty of divine portents and dramatic acts of might associated with the time of the crucifixion, let alone the undeniable power unleashed in the resurrection itself. The sweep of the synoptic storyline belies the caricatured attempts of some Muslim critics to paint the Jesus of the gospels as weak and pathetic, not least in his Gethsemane-travail.

Much about the Passion is surprising and counter-intuitive; divine victory by which the cosmic powers are set down comes through the humble submission and suffering of the Messiah. Nonetheless, the mission of the Son climaxing at the cross is indeed an expression of God's own power. The Son came to *destroy the works of the Evil One*, and "now" (at the cross) the "ruler of this world" is driven out (1 Jn 2:8; Jn 12:31-32). God (and Christ) as divine warrior is an Old Testament theme repeatedly attested in the New Testament, not least in John's apocalypse where the conquering warrior is simultaneously the "slain lamb." In the Pauline witness, the armour of God is closely related to that of the Messiah himself, the one who ultimately disarms death.[42]

Jesus meekly riding a foal into Jerusalem, soon to die, stands in quite some contrast to the trajectory of Muhammad's biography (the *sira*) wherein he rides into Mecca in "manifest triumph," assuming the reigns of political power and laying the foundations for the Muslim empire.[43] Muhammad's travail was real enough, but it ultimately had to end in a "manifest triumph" on the political and temporal plane.[44] All too often the Islamic complaint against the cross has been its alleged "passivity," its weakness and failure in terms of "might unfurled for the right."[45] Nonetheless, it *is* Christ's path down the *Via Dolorosa* which eventuates in Jesus conquering

---

[41] Witness his executioner's *volte-face* (Mk 15:39).

[42] Rom. 13:12-14; 2 Cor. 6:7; Eph. 6:1f.; 1 Thess. 5:8-10; 1 Cor. 15:55 citing Old Testament prophecy.

[43] The contrast is rather striking even on so mild and favourable (to Muhammad) a telling of the story of the "submission of Mecca" as W. Montgomery Watt's *Muhammad: Prophet and Statesman*, Oxford: Oxford University Press, 1974, p203-207.

[44] Cf. *Jesus and the Muslim*, p173.

[45] The classic historian, Ibn Khaldun (d. 1406) may even be seen to chide Jesus for failing to give rein to the impulse of prestige and power befitting the prophetic calling. See Kenneth Cragg, "The Cross and Power: The Parting of the Ways," in *Jesus and the Cross*, D. Singh, (ed.), Eugene, OR: Wipf and Stock, 2008, p42.

hell and the grave for us all. The resurrection is, of course, vital,[46] but the path to victory had to proceed by way of Golgotha. Upsetting all historical experience and cultural norms, Christ's cross becomes a sign of victory, *the victory of the one suspended on it.*

The Gospel unleashes the "power" of God to save (Rom. 1:16): the crucifixion (and resurrection) was a shocking, brilliant, and unanticipated *tour-de-force*, an act of *power* by which God disarmed evil, and overturned sin, death, and rebellion. [47] It is important to use a wide angle lens on the cross, so as to capture the breadth of its significance in the New Testament *kerygma*. The Christus Victor construct is vital to the picture. And this emphasis on "power" in the cross may be all the more relevant in our approach to Islam.

Power: Divine Will and Divine Love

Temple Gairdner makes a strong case for "power" in the Cross, the power of God's love.[48] But, strength and power as concepts are not always univocal. There is "power," and then there is "power." Garidner takes aim in particular at the sort of arbitrary power he discerns in classical Islamic discourse on a God whose essence is assumed to be permanently inaccessible.[49] (One might note that of the seven attributes of God classically enumerated in Islamic theology both "power" and "will" are prominent; love is not.[50]) In

---

[46] Rom. 1:3-4; 4:25. Cf. Zahniser, *Mission and Death*, p234-235.

[47] Paradoxically, the cross reveals divine glory. Think of the tying together of "glory" and "being lifted up" in the Gospel of John, where the latter phrase points, in the first instance, to the crucifixion.

[48] Gairdner's ideas merit consideration even if his style of discourse is unrestrained and aggressive by contemporary standards.

[49] A certain style of Muslim thought seeks to safeguard God's independence, transcendence, and freedom by emphasizing his power, will, and inscrutable nature *to the detriment of ethical categories*, heightening insecurity with respect to human destiny. See, for example, Sweetman, *Islam and Christian Theology* 2.2, London: Lutterworth, 1967, p21, 30-31, 59-60, 105, 112-114, 207, 217, 320; See Ibn Rushd's critique of the "kalamists" on this point on p169-174. Cragg's warning about extremism in Muslim anti-analogical thought about God (*al-mukhalafa*) is well put in "Tafsir and Istifsar in the Qur'an," *ICMR* 8.3, 1997, p313. Issues of a similar nature are not, of course, alien to Christian thought; think of the so-called "intellectualist" and "voluntarist" positions in Medieval theology.

[50] See Al-Ghazali's *Ihya' 'Ulum al-Din* as cited by J.W. Sweetman, *Islam and Christian Theology*, 2.2, p29, n 1 (cf. p105f.).

Islam there is a theological tendency to nominally uphold God's attributes while making them functionally inaccessible, screened off by a relentless determinism—a radically unfettered *will*.[51]

For Gairdner the strength and power of God cannot be adequately discussed until both the actual, vital character of God and the predicament of humanity are rightly understood (again, questions of worldview and ontology). And so, the "emotions" or attributes of God (wrath, love, mercy) are in fact commensurate with the stance of a loving, holy, moral being towards flawed but potentially restored creatures made in his image.[52] All of these "emotions" or "attitudes" of God must cohere together, unless we perceive God as pure volitional force, a remote essence, unmoved either by the beatitude or damnation of humans.[53]

God must be understood as truly (if not exhaustively) revealed in his attributes, particularly those of holiness and love.

We see then that "love" and "holiness"… [are] two sides of one and the same thing… The relations of God in Heaven to man are determined by [these two]… and led to Calvary's cross.[54]

In the cross of Christ we encounter the overwhelming "power" of God's love, but power appropriate to what Gairdner calls "moral" categories rather than approximating to raw force. The redemption of man requires a moral victory, not a victory of sheer force. Sin must be able to "do its worst" and so be defeated.[55]

In that which Muslim eyes regard as weakness, Christian eyes see power! What the Muslim admires as power seems to the Christian

---

[51] Progressive Muslim thinkers would demur, pushing hard for a characterization of God as consistently just, at least in the Qur'an, if not in later theology and popular thought. See Rahman, *Major Themes*, p18-24. See also Cragg's reference to Daud Rahbar's *God of Justice*, in "Tafsir and Istifsar," p312-313. The motif of "justice" runs throughout Nasr Abu Zaid (with Esther Nelson), *Voice of an Exile: Reflections on Islam*, Westport, CT: Praeger, 2004. Cf. Abdullah Saeed, *Islamic Thought: An Introduction*, New York: Taylor and Francis, 2006, p30-32, 150-152 and Sweetman, *Islam and Christian Theology* 2.2, p64-65.

[52] And, after all, the Qur'an does employ descriptions of God which allow for wrath and even compassion and mercy.

[53] See W.H.T. Gairdner, *God As Triune, Creator, Incarnate, Atoner*, Madras: Christian Literature Society for India, 1916, p58f.

[54] *God as Triune*, p55-56.

[55] See *God as Triune*, p51-54, 62-63.

under certain circumstances as sheer weakness—the weakness of the blundering giant who displays his force in a delicate moral case where it is utterly out of place. All these differences of view culminate in the Cross, which (rather than the Incarnation) is the real battle-ground between the two faiths. To the Muslim... the Cross is a blasphemy, the very embodiment of weakness and defeat; to the Christian it is the very symbol of moral strength and victory, and through it he has learned to say "the weakness of God is stronger than men."[56]

This is a power which undergoes "the worst that we can do in sinfulness and for that very reason masters it without remainder," accomplishing our forgiveness... That power is love.[57]

The Cross, Suffering, and the Power of Love

The cross is what happens when a love like Jesus' encounters a world like ours.[58] In the cross we see the divine love, a love that suffers and, strangely, expresses the very power of God. This love, received by the community of Christ, must also be a love expressed *by* that same community. So, what is lacking in the sufferings of Jesus is not their efficacy but their imitation (Col. 1:24).[59] The fact of our redemption in the cross calls all who are "in Christ" to emulation, to a cross-shaped existence of love, sacrifice, and even death as the Lord ushers in his Kingdom.[60]

The redemption purchased at the cross is participatory and transformative for the believer (cf. Gal. 2:19b-20).[61]

The early Church summarized this Scriptural mystery [of our salvation] with simple formulas like "for us and for our salvation, he came down from heaven," and "we believe in the forgiveness of

---

[56] *God as Triune*, p54.

[57] *Jesus and the Muslim*, p179.

[58] Adapting Ida Glaser's citation of Cragg ("Cross-Reference Theology," p153). Compare Cragg, *Jesus and the Muslim*, p180-183.

[59] *Jesus and the Muslim*, p183 (wording slightly altered); there Cragg also speaks of a "love that suffers."

[60] Mk 8:31-38; Jn 20:21; 1 Cor. 1:10-2.5; Gal. 6:14-15; Phil. 2:5-11.

[61] References to participation with Christ, being "in Christ," in Paul are commonly integral to passages of ethical exhortation.

sins." The vocation of the evangelist or preacher is not to analyse the mystery in detail, but to discern what mode of communication will connect to the context of the hearer, and in doing so to move more deeply into the salvific fellowship of Trinity.[62]

The love that "compels us"[63] flows from that epicenter of our very existence as God's people: The Cross of Christ. A long and costly discipleship in the way of the cross (adapting Islamic idiom, *fi sabil as-salib*) is part of the answer to the wrong, injustice, and sin in our world. More than any argument, what the Muslim world needs to encounter in the church is the cruciform, self-emptying love of Christ. The narrative of the cross is at its most compelling, most coherent, *and most powerful* in the testimony of lives changed. By his wounds we are healed, and like the redeemed of Revelation standing on the further shore of redemption, our response is not to present a didactic explanation, but to erupt in grateful worship (Rev. 5:6f.; 7:9f.; 15:1-4).

APPENDIX:

"A RESPONSE TO THE DOCTRINE OF THE CROSS."[64]

The material translated here is only a segment of Rida's long commentary on Q 4.157f. and response to Christian soteriology.

"Whoever believes in rational evidence cannot accept this [Christian redemption] story if, as no doubt, the Creator of the world is all knowing, and wise in all he creates. For this tale requires ignorance and an origin on the part of the great Creator God. As if, when he created Adam, he did not know what would happen with him (*ma yakun 'alayhi amrahu*); and when Adam transgressed, [God] did not know what justice and mercy required in that case (*sha'nihi*), until he finally came upon the solution

---

62 Personal communication from Duane Alexander Miller.
63 2 Cor. 5:14-15.

64 *Tafsir al-Manar* by Muhammad 'Abduh and Rashid Rida (this segment by Rida). (http://www.altafsir.com/Tafasir.asp?tMadhNo=0&tTafsirNo=103&tSoraNo=4&tAyahNo= 157&tDisplay=yes&Page=12&Size=1&LanguageId=1 [advancing from this web page to the following one, using the internal paging function], accessed 15 July 2015). Thanks to Azar Ajaj for his input on my translation.

(*ihtada*) after thousands of years had passed in the created order. It implies an ignorance of how to combine both these attributes from among his attributes--and being caught in the problem of the contradiction between them.

Those in the [Christian] religion accept things which are contrary to reason, and [its believers] accept from the proponents of this faith whatever is transmitted from those who supposedly did miracles, claiming to believe in it even if not understanding it ... And among the things transmitted in their first religious book (Genesis) is this sentence (6.6): "The Lord regretted that he had made humankind on the earth and was sorry in his heart." God be exalted far above all that!

Whoever accepts this [salvation] story is required to surrender to what every independent mind would reject as impossible, that the creator of the universe should become incarnate in the womb of a woman on this earth which is accounted as less than an atom by comparison with the rest of his realm and with the heavens you see from this earth. And then to become human, to eat, drink, tire, and undergo whatever else humans experience. And then his enemies take him by force and abuse and crucify him with the thieves, and make him cursed according to the ruling of a scripture which he gave to some of his messengers. God Most High be exalted above all that!

This story requires that the All-knowing, wise Creator willed something (only) after thousands of years of mulling it over and that thing was not even achieved; that is, humanity is not actually saved and rescued from punishment by the event of the crucifixion. They say that their salvation depends on faith in this story, but they do not believe the story themselves. We say: No one believes this story, for in fact "faith" confirms "reason"... and reason cannot comprehend [this story]. Those who say that they believe in it say with their tongues that which is not in their hearts, as they imitate those who dictated [this belief] to them.

For were we to [possibly] consider this sort of confession as "faith," we would say that most of humanity does not confess it, but rather rebut it by rational proofs, or some by revealed proofs, from a religion originally confirmed to them by rational proofs.[65]   And there are those who do not even know this story, and there are those who tell a similar story of other gods. So, if God were to punish them in the hereafter, not admitting them to his kingdom-- as the Christians claim--he would not be merciful based on the foundation [touted by] the missionaries, i.e. the crucifixion and the cross. So how could he combine justice and mercy thereby?

This story requires something even worse than attributing to the Creator the inability to accomplish his will in bringing together justice and mercy; that is, [the story requires] the total eradication of justice and mercy in the crucifixion of the Messiah for God punished him as a human not deserving punishment, for he was in no way guilty. So his punishment on the cross and piercing by lances [as they claim] produces neither One just nor merciful. How could it be that the Creator is neither just nor merciful, or being just and merciful that he should create a creature and place him in the dilemma of having to eradicate one of these two attributes, in trying to combine the two, losing them both?!

If then all who confess this doctrine or story are saved from the punishments of the hereafter, what then of their character and actions?   It would follow from this that the partisans of this teaching would be libertines. And the evildoer who transgresses against the wealth or persons or honour [= women?] of people, and causes corruption in the earth, and destroys crops and cattle [cf. Q 2:205]--he would be among the people of the Kingdom of the Most High, not punished for his evil and sins, and not required to account for them at all. So, if [such a one] can act according to his whims in this world, safe from the judgment of God, never mind that he is corrupt...; or, if he *is* punished for his evil and sins just like the remainder of non-Christians [lit.: non-Cross People], then what is the distinction [or "benefit"] in this doctrine?   And if he has a privilege before God Most High with respect to the [judgment], then where is the divine justice in that?

We have never seen anyone of the intelligent or the scholars of the law and regulations say that a man's forgiving the one who wronged him, or the lord's forgiving a slave who transgressed

---

[65] Presumably Rida is referring to Islam here.

against him, contradicts justice and perfection--rather they count forgiveness as among the greatest of virtues, and you see true believers in God from multiple nations describing him as forgiving and saying that he is qualified to forgive; but the claim of the Cross People that forgiveness and forbearance contradict justice is quite unacceptable."

GLOSSARY:

HINDU AND BUDDHIST WORDS

Advaita	An ancient Hindu tradition of scriptural exegesis and religious practice
Artha	Wealth
Ahisma	Principle of non-violence
Apastamba	Lived 6/5th century BC, from a family of Brahmins of a branch of the Vedic school dedicated to the study of the *Yajurveda*
Aranyakas	Expositions of the *Vedas* from approximately 8th century BC.
Ashrama	One of four age-based life stages discussed in ancient and medieval era Indian texts: a facet of Dharma
Atharva Veda	Part of the Veda: Considered part of the Hindu Canon of Scripture
Atman	Soul: one's inner self: later for some became identified with the Brahman
Bhagavad Gita	Considered part of the Hindu Canon of Scripture. Part of the Mahabharata Hindu epic
Bhakti Hinduism	A Hindu cult which considers devotional worship obligatory
Bhikkhus	An ordained monastic ("monk") in Buddhism. A female monastic ("nun") is called a *bhikkhuni*
Brahman	Considered the supreme Being, the Ultimate, Absolute Truth
Brahmana Texts	Considered part of the Hindu Canon of Scripture; composed approx. 900-700BC
Brahmin (Brahman)	The highest Hindu caste, some of whom also have priestly duties
Dhammapada	A collection of the sayings of Buddha created

193

	shortly after his death
Dharma	Duty and obligation: acting rightly
Dharma Sutras	Manuals of human conduct that form the earliest source of Hindu law.
Duhkha/Dukkha	Joy or suffering that results from one's actions
Hare Krishna	A western based sect of Hinduism
Kama	Fulfilment of desire
Karma	The cause and effect of one's behaviour which influences the future of one's life In Buddhism *karma* also incorporates a moral dimension
Karma yoga	Sets down a path of conforming to God's will through activity and deeds
Kshatriya	Traditionally the military or ruling class.
Laws of Manu	An ancient legal text: considered part of the Hindu Canon of Scripture
Mantra	A sacred saying which is repeated as part of worship; sometimes used to conjure up magical supernatural powers; also used for gaining power over others and things
Mahabharata	A Hindu epic
Maya	In Hindu philosophy, it means "illusion" and in Hindu mythology, it is also an alternate name of the Hindu goddess *Durga*
Meme theory	A theory relating to the spread of ideas between peoples and cultures
Moksha	Liberation from worldly desires and bondages: liberation from the cycles of rebirth
Purusharthas	The main goals of human life: *dharma* (righteousness), *artha* (wealth), *kama* (desire) and *moshka* (liberation from worldly desires and bondages)
Prakriti	Perishable physical human
Prasada	Offering food to a deity and then distributing it among fellow worshippers
Prayopavesa	To fast to death.
Puja	Worship; paying one's respect to a god
Purana Texts	A series of texts considered part of the Hindu Canon of Scripture; composed approx. 4th century BC to 1000AD.
Rig Veda	Part of the Veda: considered part of the Hindu

	Canon of Scripture
Samsara	The ongoing cycle of rebirth
Sanatana dharma	Denotes the "eternal" or absolute set of duties or religiously ordained practices incumbent upon all Hindus, regardless of class, caste, or sect.
Smriti	Oral traditions that have been written down
Smriti Dharmasastra	Duties to preserve the social order; law codes of Hinduism
Sramanas	Ascetics
Sruti (Shruti)	Sourced directly from the divine; sacred texts
Sutra(s)	Texts that were written down in books of palm leaves sewn together with thread as opposed to oral sayings that have been collected
Tantric Hinduism	A cult within Hinduism
Upanishads	Considered part of the Hindu Canon of Scripture; composed approx. 800-400BC
Vaishyas	Traditionally composed of the merchant class, also involved in productive labour such as agriculture
Varna	The status or caste system whereby groups are organised and hierarchy exists. *Varna* is organised by birth, family groups, heritage and social status.
Vedic texts	From Veda; Sacred text composed approx. 1500-1000BC
Yajamana	Sacrifice: one who offers a sacrifice
Yoga	Form of worship: considered as necessary for achieving a divine experience of God

Notes for Contributors

Submission requirements:

Manuscript
- Papers should not exceed 5000 (not including footnotes) words, although the Editor retains the discretion to publish papers beyond this length.
- It is preferable that submissions be prepared in Microsoft Word format.
- All papers are to be written in English, and an English transliteration given to any quotations or short phrases in original language.
- Authors are advised to use gender inclusive and non-discriminatory language.
- Any visuals should be integrated into the document, or sent separately as separate jpg or gif files with an explanation as to their position in the paper.
- Footnotes should follow the style used in previous issues of this Occasional Paper series. Please ensure that the first reference to any work in the footnotes includes all bibliographic detail. Also note that footnotes should constitute no more than an extra 25% of the word total. (That is 1250 words in footnotes for 5000 words.)
- All internet references need to include the date the material was cited. eg:
  http://www.nameofsite/nameofsection, cited dd/mm/yy

Submission
- Papers to be considered for inclusion are to be submitted directly to the Editor.
- Submissions are to be forwarded via electronic mail to csiof@mst.edu.au. If submitting within Australia, a hard copy must also be posted to CSIOF, PO Box 6257, Vermont Sth., Vic 3133.

- A declaration that the submitted articles are your own work and that you've acknowledged the work/s of others used in the articles in the references, etc. must be included with any submission.
- A covering letter that includes the authors' names, titles, affiliations, with complete mailing addresses, including email, telephone and facsimile numbers should be attached to the paper.

Review of Submissions
- All submissions will be sent to referees for anonymous recommendation.
- The Editor holds the right to make editorial corrections to accepted submissions.

Copyright
- The CSIOF Occasional Papers series is published by the Melbourne School of Theology Press. The copyright for any published papers will remain with the author. MST publishes these papers on the following conditions:

- They do not appear elsewhere (including web pages) for 180 days from the date of publication in the CSIOF Occasional Papers series.

- Whenever they are printed elsewhere (including web pages), the following notice will be included: "This article first appeared in the __ issue of the CSIOF Occasional Papers series".

- We retain the right to use the paper in any CSIOF publications, reprints, or in electronic form (ie. Online, CD-Rom, etc.).

- We retain the right to use a portion or description of the paper with your name in our promotional material.

- Authors are themselves responsible for obtaining permission to reproduce copyright material from other sources.

- The author will be presented with six copies of the publication.

www.ingramcontent.com/pod-product-compliance
Lightning Source LLC
Chambersburg PA
CBHW072129020426
42334CB00018B/1727